Experimenting with AVR Microcontrollers

Alan Trevennor

Apress®

Experimenting with AVR Microcontrollers

ISBN-13 (pbk): 978-1-4842-0902-8

ISBN-13 (electronic): 978-1-4842-0901-1

Managing Director: Welmoed Spahr
Lead Editor: Michelle Lowman
Development Editor: Douglas Pundick
Technical Reviewer: Cliff Wootton
Editorial Board: Steve Anglin, Mark Beckner, Gary Cornell, Louise Corrigan, Jim DeWolf, Jonathan Gennick, Robert Hutchinson, Michelle Lowman, James Markham, Matthew Moodie, Jeff Olson, Jeffrey Pepper, Douglas Pundick, Ben Renow-Clarke, Gwenan Spearing, Matt Wade, Steve Weiss
Coordinating Editor: Kevin Walter
Compositor: SPi Global
Indexer: SPi Global
Artist: SPi Global
Cover Designer: Anna Ishchenko

Distributed to the book trade worldwide by Springer Science+Business Media New York, 233 Spring Street, 6th Floor, New York, NY 10013. Phone 1-800-SPRINGER, fax (201) 348-4505, e-mail orders-ny@springer-sbm.com, or visit www.springeronline.com. Apress Media, LLC is a California LLC and the sole member (owner) is Springer Science + Business Media Finance Inc (SSBM Finance Inc). SSBM Finance Inc is a **Delaware** corporation.

For information on translations, please e-mail rights@apress.com, or visit www.apress.com.

Apress and friends of ED books may be purchased in bulk for academic, corporate, or promotional use. eBook versions and licenses are also available for most titles. For more information, reference our Special Bulk Sales–eBook Licensing web page at www.apress.com/bulk-sales.

Any source code or other supplementary materials referenced by the author in this text is available to readers at www.apress.com. For detailed information about how to locate your book's source code, go to www.apress.com/source-code/.

"To Wendy, who made it all possible."

Contents at a Glance

Contents

About the Author

Alan Trevennor ioriginally wanted to work in music radio. However, after getting hooked on digital electronics via a Science of Cambridge MK14 computer kit, he joined the UK computer industry in 1980 as a hardware engineer, fixing DEC PDP-11 systems.

In the 1980s he wrote hardware-related books about operating systems and Amstrad computers. He progressed to systems engineering and became a key member of DEC's UK Unix support team. He created and taught many training courses and user guides for DEC's Unix-related products, RISC computers, TCP/IP networking, and other subjects. He also contributed technical articles to many magazines.

In the 1990s Alan migrated to being a digital media solutions architect with Compaq and then HP. From then until he left HP in 2009, Alan worked on digital media technical solutions and business consultancies. He worked for customers as diverse as the BBC, Reuters, Allied Domecq Leisure, BT, Music Choice, The National Trust, RBS, Glaxo, Virgin Radio, and Nokia. Coming full circle, he later spent a great deal of time in music radio stations as part of a team working on a joint HP/Nokia project—Visual Radio. During an incredibly varied career, Alan has created numerous technical solutions (some using AVR microcontrollers) as well as large amounts of user training materials and documentation.

Alan now lives in Cornwall, UK with his wife and son. He runs a "hobby" business part time and works full time as a technical author for Microtest, a creator and supplier of advanced medical software based in Cornwall.

About the Technical Reviewer

Cliff Wootton is a former Interactive TV systems architect at BBC News.

The "News Loops" service developed there was nominated for a BAFTA and won a Royal Television Society Award for Technical Innovation. He is an invited speaker on pre-processing for video compression at the Apple WWDC conference. He also taught postgraduate MA students about real-world computing, multimedia, video compression, metadata, and researching the deployment of next-generation interactive TV systems based on open standards.

He is currently working on R&D projects investigating new interactive TV technologies, involved with MPEG standards working groups, writing more books on the topic, and speaking at conferences when not lecturing on multimedia at the University of the Arts in London.

Introduction

> *(Stephen Leacock)* *"Writing is not hard. Just get paper and pencil, sit down, and write as it occurs to you. The writing is easy—it's the occurring that's hard."*

I think microcontrollers can be a bit like that. You have a world of possibility—a blank page if you will—and you can combine the intelligence of your MCU, your own imagination, and the fantastic toolkits you have at your disposal to build pretty much whatever you can imagine. But, what will you build?

For some people, amassing the tools and the parts to build MCU projects can turn out to be most of the fun. Like a "wannabe" chef who spends ages sharpening knives, polishing silverware, and finding neat and tidy places for every little implement, it's easy to get mesmerized by the tools and the processes and lose sight of what it's all for. For other people it's the other way around: they have a plethora of ideas, but no clear idea how to break the overall task down into manageable steps to make it happen.

Here, our focus is definitely on the "what." - as in "What can I build with all these great tools and techniques?". We're going to run through a number of projects, small ones and not so small ones. My hope is that, even if you don't want to build these projects they will help you create ideas of your own. I also hope you'll gain a few perspectives on the different activities concerned with MCU projects and their possible sequencing. Another possible side effect may be that you'll start to see the contents of your plastics and cardboard recycling bin in a whole new way!.

Project Bases

In most projects in this book you have a simple choice about what base to build upon. The choices are one of the following:

- Building the project on a breadboard with an attached AVR programmer.

- Building the project on a piece of solder board of some kind (see the "Duck Shooter" game for an example of doing it this way).

- Using a freeware package like Eagle or Fritzing to design a printed circuit board for the project and building your version of the project onto that. Of course, this can be quite an expensive option, although the software mentioned is free (and there are other free software packages, too), when you use them to design a PCB you still have to pay someone to make your circuit board from the design that is produced by the package.

Deciding which project to build in which way is going to be largely determined by whether you regard the project in question as a "keeper" project. In other words, do you plan to build up the project, get it working, stand back in awe of its wondrousness for a while, and then tear it down and reuse the components for something new? Or, do you plan to deploy the project to your home, your office, or your car as a permanent fixture? If the former, then you'll want to build the project on a breadboard. If the latter, then you'll want to build your project on something that you can build into a box and have it become a piece of "set and forget" infrastructure in your home or office.

Whatever method you use it's very important that you include the all-important ISP connector for updating the MCU software so that you can make changes to the software as needed. You want to avoid a situation where you use a stand-alone programmer and have to keep moving the MCU chip between project and programmer. So, it's your decision as to what base you use for the electronics side of the projects. The circuit diagrams mostly assume you'll be building a custom board, so if you're building on a breadboard you'll need to do some small amount of adapatations around power supply arrangements.

Project Chapter Formats

In general, the format of each project chapter is

- A description of the project: what it does, why you might want to build it.

- A design discussion, detailing the trade-offs and features of the design.

- A "maker" section, which deals with how to make any mechanical elements of the project and some pointers to where you might find the parts you need.

- A circuit diagram for the electronic aspects of the project (including the MCU).

- Details of the project software. In most cases the software is too long to reproduce in full, so there is a summary of the software and the full software listing is available for download.

- A code walk of the software that names all the software's functions and provides a short commentary about what each one does. This code walk is intended to help you understand the full software listing when you download it from the book's web site (http://www.apress.com/9781430244462).

Each project is illustrated with diagrams and photos that should help you build one of your own or more likely, make your own version of it. Even if you start by building the project as presented here, you'll learn a lot more from modifying it later on to meet your own needs. In many cases you'll probably make improvements or enhancements to my original design in the process of customization.

A quick word on legibility... the difficulty of legibly reproducing circuit diagrams with lots of fine detail in a printed form is something that authors and publishers have always struggled with. Fortunately, the Internet makes it possible to offer you an alternative. If there is detail in a circuit diagram that you can't make out in this book, go to the book's web site where you will find electronic versions of all the diagrams in formats that will enable you to enlarge details that may be hard to see on the page. As mentioned previously, the full software listings are available on the web site too.

All the circuit diagrams have been reproduced here from my original completed designs, so they should work for you just as well as they did for me. However, if you find any mistakes please let me know via the publisher, so that we can verify the error and put corrections on the web site to help other people. Similarly, if any components or parts used in the projects should become unavailable between the writing of this book and when you need them, we will put information on the web site about possible workarounds or replacement products that may serve the same purpose.

Whilst working with electronics, be aware of static electricity. Get yourself an anti-static work mat and wrist band if you can. Think about this. You'll have had a static shock yourself at some stage, perhaps from a car door, from a door handle, or from touching some piece of earthed equipment. So you, at whatever size you are, can get static electricity shocks from things. But in fact, you get static shocks all day every day from many things; it's just that most of them are much too small to register with your nervous system. But now, reflect that you are handling chips that have millions of transistors inside them, many of which are less than one millionth of an inch across. On that scale, the tiny shocks that you don't even notice seem like lightning bolts to those tiny components and can destroy or weaken them in an instant.

Of course, most modern semiconductors have a certain degree of inbuilt static protection on their external pin connections, but we need to help things along by being aware that we bring static electricity to the work bench with us and generate more while we're working. So, using an anti-static kit is a good habit to get into. Don't get paranoid about static, but don't pretend it doesn't exist: You may not zap your semiconductors outright, but a lack of static control can shorten their life span and/or make them operate unreliably.

Finally, please **work safely**. You are dealing with electricity in these projects and electricity should always be treated with respect; even if you are only dealing with 5 volts, respect and care should be the watchwords. Ensure that your power supply is a safe one. It should be appropriately fused on the mains side and on the DC output side. Inappropriate fuse values are a major safety hazard. Fitting a 10 amp fuse to a device that only ever uses 1 amp is crazy and potentially dangerous: if a fault occurs in the device then it could heat up nicely and even catch fire before it blows the fuse. Try to fuse your devices at no more than what they need plus perhaps 10% extra. Appropriate AC-side fusing should ensure that, should anything go wrong, you'll have a dead device on your hands, not a house fire. Appropriate DC-side fusing might make the difference between having to replace the fuse and having to replace a whole board full of components.

When you are soldering, wear goggles if you can, to protect your eyes from the smoke. Always make sure your work area is well ventilated so that you don't have to breathe in the solder fumes and smoke; use a desk fan set on low to waft smoke away toward an open window. Use a soldering iron that has some kind of holster or holder so that you don't burn holes in your carpets, furniture, clothes or yourself! Never, ever flick solder around; it stays hot for a long time after it leaves the iron. If you need to remove solder from the iron, use a damp (but not wet) ball of tissue paper or scrap cotton material.

If you need to remove solder from your project board (e.g., because you put a little too much on and it has bridged two contacts when you didn't mean for that to happen), get yourself a solder sucker. These are quite cheap to buy, and provide a manually operated suction pump with a heat-resistant tip that can be used to suck molten solder away from a board.

So, work safe, use a helping-hands project gripper if you have one and be sensible and very careful about soldering iron usage.

Project Scope and Difficulty

The projects are presented in no particular order. Some of the projects are large and some are small. They're also of various types—some are purely electronic, but many include some degree of "makery"—using easy-to-get materials (such as stick wood) or adapting or reusing stuff such as discarded plastic packaging or materials.

So, if you have a preference for starting with, say, a simple project, choose one that you can build up on a breadboard. If you're inclined to build something that has more of a mechanical element to it, you'll probably want to start with a project like the sliding panel, which is heavier on construction and not so heavy on electronics.

The simple fact is that the only thing that the projects truly have in common is that there is an AVR embedded in each and every one. But, that's why we're here! I hope you build at least one of the projects, or at least that you enjoy reading about them all.

CHAPTER 1

▨ ▨ ▨

Project 1: Good Evening, Mr. Bond: Your Secret Panel

We're in at the deep end with this project. There is some fairly complicated mechanical making and woodwork in this project. There is no reason at all why you should do this project first, so if it seems a bit daunting and you want to build up to it, have a look at some of the simpler projects first.

This project celebrates that old favorite of certain movie and story genres–the secret panel–the kind of panel that unexpectedly opens in the wood paneling of a classic country house library when you touch the contacts embedded in both eyes of a portrait on the wall, or turn the head of an apparently immobile statue! But what's behind the panel . . .? Well, that's rather up to you.

A Life Ruined by Movies and TV

I admit it. When I was younger, I watched way too much Batman, Thunderbirds, Scooby Doo, Secret Service movies, and body-in-the-library mysteries. Mystery and secrets are the themes that tie these entertainments together. All of them (at one time or another) featured a secret door or a secret panel, inside which was variously concealed an underground silo full of advanced technology, a crazy janitor named Jameson, a control panel with switches marked "Launch Missiles," or a bloodstained murder weapon. I always wanted a reason to have secret panel in my own house, but I always struggled to think of a use for it in my own real life.

The shameful truth is that, if I'm honest, I *still* struggle to think of what I am really going to use it for–but the good news is that now that I have built my "secret panel," I will finally have to give it some serious thought!

Making It Real

Oh boy, there are so many ways to do this, but the most obvious ones are not necessarily the best. Let's start by stating the basic requirements, which are these:

- A small panel is to be dragged about 9–12 inches and back again by using an electric motor under the control of an MCU.

- The panel must slide smoothly (but not too quickly, you want to savor the moment of movement and revelation) between its open and closed positions.

- The panel must always return to the same open and closed positions; these positions cannot vary by more than very small amounts.

- The panel must be of a size that is easily concealed, or it must blend in as much as possible with whatever it is set into.

- The panel must only be activated by a concealed activation method (a hidden button, etc.).

- The secret panel assembly as a whole must operate in vertical or horizontal orientation. It must be able to be set in a wall or into a desk.

- The panel should be safe–that is, its mechanism should not be strong enough to cut off somebody's finger!

- The panel, when it opens, must reveal something utterly astounding!

I'm afraid that although I have some ideas, the revelation is mostly going to be up to you!

The Fireline Fiasco

My first attempt at this project involved a convoluted system of pulleys and used fireline (a very strong plastic thread that's used for jewelry and fishing line) which allowed a single motor with two spools to push *and* pull the panel into position (see Figure 1-1).

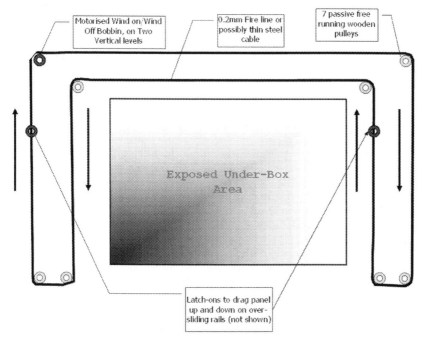

Figure 1-1. *Thread and pulley version (failed)*

This worked pretty well, but only for about a day! It turns out that fireline, at least for this use, stretches slightly and with a fairly long run like this, it meant that the push-pull motor arrangement (top left in the diagram) was not viable since the thread got progressively longer and thus looser. After a day or so of use, it got slack enough to jump off the winding spools and wreck the whole scheme!

Next, I tried using some steel garden wire in place of the fireline, but this idea was a nonstarter with the motors that I had on hand. Steel garden wire is not very flexible, and when used with the required number of right-angled turns, it exerted more drag than the motor could handle. With a more powerful motor and a slightly thinner wire, this idea might work. The other problem that I became aware of, before I gave up on this approach, was that the wooden pulleys (I used the same arrangement as described in the Solenoid leverage example in Chapter 4 of *Practical AVR Microcontrollers* [Apress, 2012]) started to chew through the wooden mount and go off the true when subjected to the force required. So, no prize for this approach! I have no doubt that with a metal frame, some metal pulleys with smooth bearings, and a powerful motor, it probably could work, but it would get pretty expensive, pretty fast!

My next idea was a simple one. The panel is pulled open by the motor, again just using fireline threads. Then, when the motor turns the other way, a counterbalancing weight pulls the panel from the other end to return it to the closed position. Since, in this arrangement, the fireline is not pushing *and* pulling, it doesn't matter if it stretches a little. However, this scheme would presuppose that the panel will be mounted in a place where there would be space for this counterbalance to travel up and down, and, actually,

I struggled to envisage many installation scenarios where that might be true. Similarly, I tried out but discounted the idea of return springs; the kind of return springs you would need would be quite long and might be hard to fit into the overall mechanism space. Also, you would have to tether the panel to the springs with something lightweight but strong, and if that something stretched . . . then again you would encounter the precision problem.

Thinking Again

The absolutely ideal solution would be a helical spring. This is the kind of rotary spring that's built into extensible measuring tapes, or extensible "queue barriers," the kind you often see in stores, museums, or stadiums. However, I tried using the helical spring from a measuring tape (the most obvious low-cost source of such a spring) and found that it's not nearly strong enough for this purpose. Springs with the kind of return force required are meant for use in things like elevator car doors, and they come with a very unattractive price tag of several hundred dollars. Curses! Foiled again!

Next, I tried some steel-threaded rod. This stuff can be bought in almost any hardware store and is used for a variety of things in the building trade. It's also pretty cheap. If you put a nut on the threaded rod and turn the rod while holding the nut still, the nut slowly moves up or down. You do have to spin the rod fairly fast to get a decent speed of movement–but the amount of force required to turn the rod is actually quite small due to the immense amount of leverage involved. So this idea was promising.

After a search on the Internet, I found that many model makers and woodworking sources have a "threaded insert," which you can put inside a block of wood and which presents an internal thread suitable for use with a threaded rod. Figure 1-2 shows one of these.

Figure 1-2. Threaded insert

This insert in Figure 1-2 has a metric M6 thread through the center–but you can get these in various metric or imperial sizes from the following sources:

- www.amazon.com (United States). Search for "threaded insert" in "Industrial and scientific" category.

- www.modelfixings.co.uk (UK).

On the outside, the insert has a coarse thread that can chew its way into a suitably sized hole through a wooden block and an Allen key head to help you screw it into the wood.

My idea was to use a couple of these fixed onto some small wood blocks on each side of the sliding panel. I built this idea up, but it has two crucial drawbacks. First, it's far, far too slow; I started with a 60 rpm motor and the panel movement was positively glacial! I tried using a 500 rpm motor, but the panel still moved too slowly. Worse (and this is the second problem), when you spin the threaded rods at that speed you really do need proper metal ball-race bearings at each end. Using holes in the wood at each end of the rod really doesn't work when those spin speeds are involved. Since these threaded rods are almost never quite straight, they generate vibration when spun at any speed–especially at the lengths required here; in short, the mechanism would shake itself apart in no time. The threads on the standard rods are too fine.

Again, there is a fix for this. You could use "Acme" threaded rods (or the similar "trapezoidal threaded" rods) and nuts. These kind of threads are much more suitable and high precision. The rods are usually thicker and the threads are more coarse, but deeper. These are intended for exactly this kind of use. If you look at the thread on a bench vise or a manual car jack, you'll likely find one of these threads in use there. The problem is that if you elect to use one of these threads you increase the cost of the project by something like an order of magnitude–they are not cheap. You'd also have to find a source of Acme or Trapezoidal threaded inserts–which I have not yet managed to do. So, this approach comes close, but it seems to run into the sand on details and cost.

Racking Up a Success

Finally, I settled on something intended for robotics or model vehicle use. There are lots of gearboxes made for driving wheeled vehicles. Here, a motor/gearbox assembly is mounted in a robot, or a model vehicle, and provides controlled drive to its wheels. If we hold such an assembly captive in a frame, and fit it with cogs instead of wheels, it can drag a panel back and forth. This is effectively a rack-and-pinion system. The panel is fitted with tracks on its underside that mesh with the cogs, as in Figure 1-3.

Figure 1-3. Sliding panel underside

Many suitable gearboxes and motor assemblies are available:

- www.pololu.com/catalog/category/34 (United States and global).

Or, for a very low-cost example–the one I used, in fact:

- www.mindsetsonline.co.uk/product_info.php?products_id=200 (UK).

You can get the rack parts from

- www.robotmarketplace.com (various products–search for rack).

- www.technobots.co.uk (search for part numbers 4600-024 and 4600-110).

The exact details of the woodwork part of this project will vary. The essential requirement is to make the panel that you want to slide and build everything else around it. The panel should be as symmetrical as you can make it, it should be as smooth and flat as you can make it, and it should be fairly lightweight. If the panel surface will be visible, it will have to match the surrounding surface if it's not to stick out like a sore thumb. If you're lucky enough to have a wood-paneled room (or, even better, be building one), you might be able to find a way to set your project into the paneling–everybody's idea of a classic secret panel.

Probably (as in my prototype), it will have to be of a size that can easily hide behind a "concealer," which might be a picture, a mirror, or a drape or wall hanging of some kind. If it's set into a horizontal surface like a desk, worktop, or shelf, it might be concealed beneath a mouse mat, a desktop CD-ROM, a blotting pad, a writing surface, an "in tray," a clock, a large ornament, a small loudspeaker, a desk tidy–really the possibilities are endless.

The sticking point is usually going to be space; you'll need space behind or under your secret panel to allow for the mechanism and the concealed compartment. Hollowing out such a space in a brick or concrete wall can be done but is problematic.

There may not be enough space back there for what you need. However, it can be a lot easier to accommodate in a less solid structure, such as the following:

- A drywall.

- A large walk-in closet or an enclosed shelving unit.

- The kind of custom cabinetry often made for a home-theatre setup.

- A desk or work surface.

Of course, always bear in mind that your panel doesn't have to be a sliding one (although that's what we're building here). It could be a flip-open panel that looks like a picture or a decorative molding; one that flips open when you activate a solenoid via your AVR.

Once you have your panel made, you need to design a frame. The frame must

- Be rigid enough to remain square and not distort when you mount it behind something else.

- Be suitable for fitting a backbox or under-box onto.

- Be suitable for mounting the motor on.

- Provide a slideway for the panel.

The photo sequence in Figures 1-4 through 1-6 shows my version of the project parts; luckily I had a drywall that I could play around with so I was able to cut a hole, right through into a closet on the other side. This meant that I could keep everything hidden from view. I'll go into some of these parts in more detail later in the chapter.

▓ **Caution**   Are you making a permanent version of this project for serious use? It's important to ensure that if the panel jams, its fuse blows, or its power supply fails, you can still access the mechanism and electronics in some way. You don't want to have to smash the thing apart if somebody fools around with it and blows the fuse. It's meant to be secure by virtue of being secret; it's not meant to be impregnable!

Figure 1-4 shows the frame for my prototype sliding panel.

The depth of the frame is driven by how deep you want the concealed compartment to be.

Note the horizontal cross-brace to ensure that the structure does not flex; thus, making the slide tracks converge or diverge along their length.

Figure 1-4. Sliding panel frame

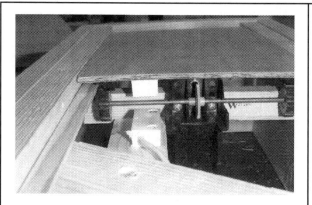

Figure 1-5. Panel drive assembly (without motor)

In Figure 1-5 you can see the panel set into the slideway and how the tracks on its underside mesh with the cogs on the axle.

Note: the motor is not yet installed in this photo. However, you can see that one of the two magnetic sensors and the magnet (enclosed in white plastic) has been installed by supergluing it to the underside of the sliding panel.

Figure 1-6. Panel drive assembly (with motor)

Here's another view of the drive mechanism. The sliding panel has been removed; you can now see the concealed compartment behind the motor assembly (see "The Secret Compartment" below for details).

The motor is now installed. In the assembly I used I found it was a good idea to use a cable tie to better bind the motor into place, since it is only a clip fit.

Hiding the Button

Of course, it's pointless to have a secret panel if you have an obvious activation button for it. So finding a nonobvious method of activating your secret panel is quite important.

You *could* just have a hidden keypad that sits alongside the panel, but that's a bit, well, tedious. In all the best movies, it just takes a finger jab at a cunningly concealed button to make the panel slide or flip open. So, where can we hide the button? I investigated several possibilities.

- Inside a figurine of "The Stig" (the mystery test driver from the BBC TV series "Top Gear"). This started out life as a novelty gift. It contained shower gel. When it was empty I decided not to throw it away but to keep it as a shelf ornament. Actually, though, having washed it out, it occurred to me that if I could thread a pair of wires through it and mount a tiny push button under Stig's removable head (the lid for the shower gel)–well, that might work!

- Inside a clock. I have a carriage clock that has its own secret compartment behind the face. How about hiding the button in there? The clock seldom needs to move, so hiding the wires is pretty easy.

- Inside a hollow book, the kind sold as a "security safe" or "book safe" on numerous web sites and stores. It's an old idea, but still a good one. The problem is the trailing wires. You could go for the additional complication of battery operation and a wireless sender inside the fake book; however, if you're really that serious about security, this would have to send an encrypted activation signal. Of course, you'd also need a receiver and decoding software at the AVR board end of things.

  Without resorting to wireless, you're going to have wires trailing when you pull the book off the shelf. You could do it another way; use a piece of reflective foil on the back of the book and a reflective sensor built into the back of the book case that recognizes when the book is removed, but that makes you dependent upon several assumptions, such as that the book will always be in the same position and that when the room is in darkness the light doesn't give away the position of the device, and so on. So, the hollow book idea is do-able, but it has a lot of snags to work out.

- A pair of touch contacts disguised as screw heads or random furniture features. I actually tried this with an old chair that had its covering fixed on with metal furniture studs. I tried wiring one stud into one of the AVR's analog inputs and the other to ground. The idea is that when you use one finger from each hand to bridge between the two, the panel opens. Unfortunately, as you can't use adjacent studs which might be discovered accidentally by anyone sitting on the chair, the cable lengths get a little too long and you get a lot of noise which can result in random activations even just because somebody walks past the chair. I also feared that it might not be long before static electricity might zap the AVR input. Somebody in nylon clothing shuffling around on a chair can probably generate quite a lot of static and that static might well want to escape through the AVR input. It might be possible to resolve these issues with a different electrical arrangement and smarter discriminating software, but it seemed like a long job and, well, there were other, more attractive, alternatives.

In the end, I built the shower gel Stig version and the clock version. Unfortunately, the owners of the Stig copyright were unable to give us permission to use pictures of that version, but take it from me, it looks very cool! The clock version (which we can show in a picture) is also pretty good. Figures 1-7 and 1-8 show the clock normally and with secret frontage opened to reveal the push-button box.

An unassuming modern-day repro carriage clock.

But this clock houses not one but two secrets!

Figure 1-7. *Just a clock*

First, it has an opening front which reveals a set of tiny storage shelves.

Second, on the bottom shelf is a tiny box with a button in it. Guess what happens when the button is pressed? Aw! you're no fund . . .

Figure 1-8. *The clock of secrets revealed!*

Position Sensors

I briefly considered the idea of using some distance sensors to allow the software to know the panel position. However, the cost of using these is not really justified here. All we really need is a momentary switch closure when the panel reaches its fully open or fully closed position. This could be done with mechanical switches with long actuation arms–as covered in "Sensing Movement" in Chapter 4 of *Practical AVR Microcontrollers* (Apress, 2012). However, I was not keen on this approach because

- I wanted to avoid anything that might impede the panel's movement, or have the potential to do so as the mechanism wears.

- Mounting physical switches on the prototype frame was actually going to be problematic.

In the end I went for a contactless approach. I found some small magnetic security sensors which used encapsulated reed switches that can detect a magnet being within about 1/2" (12 mm) of them. These products are made to be used as simple door or window sensors in alarms and security systems.

All I had to do was mount a small magnet on the lower–unseen–side of the sliding panel and mount one reed switch at the fully open point and another at the fully closed point of the panel's travel. The software is written such that it continually polls the switches whenever the panel is in motion, so it won't miss the switches being activated as the magnet passes.

These small magnet/switch products are widely available, for example

- www.amazon.com (United States) search for "magnetic window alarm sensor"–you'll find lots of examples.

- www.maplin.co.uk (UK)–search for stock number MM08, or look on B&Q web site, etc.

The Secret Compartment

When the sliding panel has slid gracefully aside, it will reveal the secret compartment. This is the nub of the whole thing–the reason for doing it; I think that means it deserves to have some magic about it!

I built a small wooden box sized to fit snugly inside the frame. I made quite a wide brim for it out of wide flat wood. Underneath the brim I put two flexible LED strips (blue ones) and fixed them on with twists of garden wire drilled through holes in the side of the box (similar to the technique used to fix the LED strips in the waterfall passageway light project).

When seen from straight on (as it normally would be once installed), you can't see the LED strips–you just see a circle of blue light fading up (thanks to the software) as the panel opens. It looks superb. Figures 1-9 and 1-10 show the backbox made and ready to be installed in the frame, with LED strips installed.

Figure 1-9. *The compartment before installing in the frame*

Figure 1-10. *The compartment showing LED strip*

Obviously if you're building one of these for yourself the size of your backbox or under-box is going to depend on how much space you have and the size of the frame. Finally, with the backbox installed in the frame, the motor fitted, and the panel in place and ready to slide we have the mechanical side of things settled; it's time to look at the electronics.

The Electronics

Figure 1-11 shows the circuit diagram for the electronics side of the secret panel project.

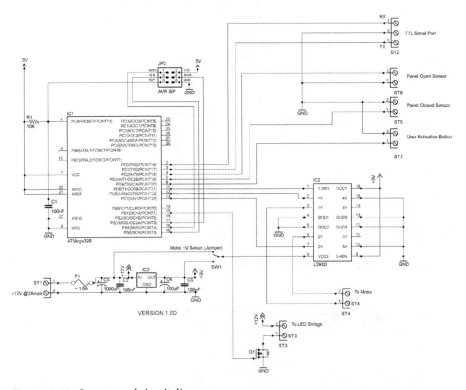

Figure 1-11. *Secret panel circuit diagram*

In my version of this project a +12-volt supply is needed for the LEDs and the +5V is derived from that using a 7805 voltage regulator. That regulator should be fitted with a heatsink. If you are using a LED string product that needs only +5V (as many SMD (surface mount device) LED strings do) and your motor is happy running on +5V, then you can simplify this design quite a lot.

▓ **Caution**   It's *very* important to make sure that you use a fuse—as indicated in the Figure 1-11—nasty things can happen if something goes wrong and there is no fuse to blow! This is especially important in any device with moving parts where fingers may get caught.

Whichever side of the power supply (12V or +5V) is running, the motor should have C3 on it. This is a fairly large capacitor, which is there to counteract the motor's startup demand. It's shown on the +12V side on the diagram, but swap around C3 and C6 if you're running your motor from +5V.

The electronics for this project consists of two chips, one voltage regulator, and one transistor. The first chip is of course our trusty ATmega328 (you could easily use ATmega168 instead if you wanted to–the code for this project is quite small). As with all our projects, the AVR has to be running at 8 MHz (as detailed in Chapter 3 of *Practical AVR Microcontrollers* [Apress, 2012]). We of course have our usual ISP jack for programming the AVR and the reset RC network across the RESET pin and we have the TTL level serial port. If you're building the circuit on the test bed breadboard (which is what I did) then you'll already have all these items. If you're building this on a solder board or some other way, you'll need to provide these things.

The second chip is an L293D chip; this was the one used in Chapter 4 of *Practical AVR Microcontrollers* (Apress, 2012) when we looked at "H" switches and push-pull drivers for use with stepper motors. Here, though, we're only using a single coil motor so we're only using half of the chip–we disable the other half. The chip can drive a motor up to about 600 ma, so you'll need to make sure that your motor is not going to overload it. The L293 does feature over current protection, though, so if you are in any doubt, try out your motor and see what happens.

Three I/O lines go from the MCU to the L293D

- AVR pin 11 (Arduino digital pin 5) connects to the enable input we are using (pin 1). The AVR has to make this pin HIGH for the L293D to be enabled.

- AVR pin 12 and pin 13 (Arduino digital pins 6 and 7, respectively) are used to set the polarity of the power going to the motor (i.e., which of the "Y" outputs is pushing and which is pulling). If they are both set to LOW then the motor gets no power. The software PWM pulses whichever is the positive lead to make the motor ramp up. The enable pin overrides these signals.

Pin 8 of the LS293D is the motor supply pin. As shown in the diagram in Figure 1-11, you can use a simple wire jumper to provide power from +5 volts or +12 volts, depending on the voltage your motor requires. The L293D spec says you can use up to +36V as the motor supply. The unused half of the L293D simply has its inputs tied to ground. We don't need to use snubber diodes or any current limiting; the chip has all that built in.

The AVR's pin 15 (Arduino digital pin 9) interfaces to the MOSFET, and that drives the LED strings. The MOSFET used is over spec for this purpose, which means that you could add a lot more LED strings to your own creation.

The two limit switches (in the software these are called PANEL_FULLY_OPEN and PANEL_FULLY_CLOSED) connect to AVR pins 4 and 5 (Arduino digital pins 2 and 3, respectively). These are simple magnet-operated reed switches which connect to ground when the magnet attached to the moving panel passes near them. The internal AVR 20K pull-ups are enabled on these pins, so there is no need for external pull-up resistors.

Finally, the user's push button (wired across from inside the clock–as shown earlier) interfaces via AVR pin 6 (Arduino digital pin 4). This is, again, a simple connection to ground with a pull-up enabled on the AVR. The software only activates this push button when it is released; this is to prevent a user from holding it down to make the panel cycle continuously, which it is not meant to do (the L293D would go over temperature and shut down, for one thing).

That's it for the electronics, all the external connections in the prototype are–as shown–made by screw connectors, but you could use something else if you wanted to. I used PCB mounting screw connectors with fairly long pins.

Sliding Panel Electronics Troubleshooting

You can find out quite a lot by connecting to the TTL level serial port (see Chapter 3 of *Practical AVR Microcontrollers* [Apress, 2012] for details) because the software outputs quite a few messages as it goes about its work. It will indicate each operation as it starts and ends; it also indicates fault conditions and sensor events.

You'll find that the reed switches used as limit detectors do tend to bounce quite a lot. The software counteracts this bounce by reacting to the first "sighting" of the limit switch it is expecting to close. For example, if the software is commanding the panel to close, it continuously monitors the fully closed sensor and reacts to the first pulse it sees from the PANEL_FULLY_CLOSED switch and then stops looking at that switch.

If you are having problems, there is provision in the software for fitting a "fault" LED provides additional assistance (it's not shown on the circuit diagram in Figure 1-11 because I never needed it and hopefully you won't either). If you want additional indication of what the MCU is doing, attach an LED with its + lead to AVR pin 14 (Arduino digital pin 8) and its negative lead through a 330R resistor to ground. When this LED lights up it means that a panel transit has taken too long. During building you'd see messages about this on the serial channel. However, once installed and working it could be handy to have an LED indicator showing there is a problem.

If the LED comes on (or you see a panel transit time-out message on the serial channel) it could be caused by several things.

- The panel is stuck due to some blockage or mechanical jam.

- You're using a slower motor than I did (in which case, adjust the time-out value MAX_PANEL_MOVE_TIME).

- You've adjusted the parameters of the ramp-up function within the software which has altered the total transit time of the motor.

In most cases you'll know if the mechanism jams; it will make a ghastly noise. If it used to work but now times out, maybe the panel slides need cleaning and are slowing down the panel movement? In my design the panel is held captive in its slides by the wall or surface onto which you fix it. If the surface has warped slightly so that it's squeezing the panel and restricting its ease of movement, that can easily cause a problem.

If you're having problems with the electronics of a newly built panel it may be because your motor has different startup characteristics than the one I used and it's spiking your power supply or momentarily dragging it down (if the power supply is not providing enough power). Such a problem can have many negative effects, such as a complete software restart whenever the motor is commanded to start, or garbled text coming out of the TTL serial port, or the motor starting for a moment then stopping again.

If you do suspect that the motor is causing problems, try modifying the rampPanelMotorUp function within the software to make a softer, more gradual, start.

If the problem remains, in many cases the answer will be to add a larger reservoir capacitor across the supply rail supplying the motor. Try duplicating the existing reservoir capacitor (in my design this would be C3) to see if that fixes the problem, or at least changes it a little which would indicate that you're on the right track and just need to increase the capacitor value. Also, try adding some duplicates of C2 and C5, placing them near the L293D. If you can, try a different power supply which offers a little more amperage, or try a different motor.

Software Commentary

The software is–downloadable from this book's web site (www.apress.com/9781430244462). The following is a code walk through the main functions of the program.

Function	Commentary
Declarations Header Section (args: none)	In this initial section the Arduino pin numbers for the various external connections are defined (see previous text) and various constants are declared. Of special interest are:
	• MAX_PANEL_MOVE_TIME which defines (in milliseconds) how many seconds the panel is given to complete its transit from open to closed (or vice versa). This is set at a default of five seconds; you should customize it for the motor you are using. Don't allow too long because if there is a problem with the mechanism or a blockage, the motor will grind away for longer than it needs to. Don't make it too short, or the software will start issuing time-outs and give up on moving the panel. The value should be about one second longer than the panel transit would normally take.
	• LED_DELAY is used to slug the LED strings fade rate so that it happens more stylishly, slowly and gracefully. Increase this value to slow the fade, or decrease it (minimum = 1) to increase.
	• limitSwStates is an array of two items which hold the latest state of the limit switches. These are updated regularly in the main loop so they are always up to date.

(*continued*)

Function	Commentary
setup() args: None	The setup() function initializes all the I/O pins as required (including enabling pull-up resistors for inputs) and initializes the serial port. It then collects the initial sensor states. Then, it fades the LED strings up and down to provide a visual verification that they are working. Finally, if the panel seems to be open, it is closed.
loop() args: None	The main loop() function of this program is pretty simple. If the user button has not been pressed then it just updates the limit switch states–and that's it! If the user switch *has* been pressed then it checks to see if the panel looks as if it is closed; if so, it opens it. In any other case (the panel is open, or neither sensor is active) the panel is closed. All user button press actions result in a message going out to the serial port.
closePanel() args: ledFaderStart AND openPanel() args: ledFaderStart	These functions command the motor to ramp up in the required direction to open or close the panel. They then wait until either the appropriate sensor is activated (e.g., closePanel waits for the PANEL_FULLY_CLOSED sensor to be hit) or a time-out occurs. The LED strings are faded in or out while waiting for the panel to complete its transit. The LEDs are left fully on (panel open) or off (panel closed) at the end of the function. The motor is always turned off when these functions end. LED fading doesn't start until ledFaderStart milliseconds after the function is called. This allows an adjustment point to allow fading and panel movement to be better synced when using different motors and processors. Messages are issued to the serial port, and the failStateLed pin is put ON in the case of a time-out.

(*continued*)

Function	Commentary
rampPanelMotorUp() args: pwmLead	This function does a feathered start on the motor. Electrically and mechanically, this works a lot better than just putting full power on the motor straight away, and in this application it looks classier!
	The function takes one argument which is pwmLead. As detailed earlier in this chapter (see "The Electronics" section earlier.) there are two control lines into the motor driver. By setting one or other of these to low and the other to high you control the polarity of the power supplied to the motor. pwmLead in this function specifies which of the possible two Arduino pin numbers is to be the positive. The polarity setup is actually done by the setMotorControls() support function.
	We initially increase the PWM pulses into the motor quite gently but more aggressively as the PWM pulses get longer. You'll probably need to tune the point at which this happens (as per comment in the code) to best suit your chosen motor.
motorOff() args: None	Sets both motor leads to LOW so that no power flows through the motor. Used to stop the motor quickly when the panel movement is over. As an alternative to this you could also add a rampPanelMotorDown() function which slow-stops the panel, but that depends on how much momentum your mechanical components have and whether they might overshoot too badly.
progressLedPwm() args: fadingUp	This function progresses a LED string fade up or down (the Boolean argument fadingUp indicates which type of activity is in progress). In order to make sure that fading is pretty and doesn't happen too fast, we use a ledDelayCtr (a static variable). This effectively counts how many times this function is called and only does a fade step every LED_DELAY calls.
Various Others	The other remaining functions are very small and self-explanatory.

All Together Now!

So, finally, it is time to put it all together. I made a hole in the drywall. On the panel side that was just large enough to let the secret compartment become visible. On the other side, it had to be big enough to mount the frame into the wall, so it was quite a large hole (but inside the closet mentioned earlier). I put a frame around the hole on the front side and secured the frame assembly on the rear side mounted so that the secret compartment lined up to be visible. After making sure that the panel could move back and forth freely, which involved a tedious amount of smoothing of the rear face of the drywall (which had to be dead flat to ensure that the panel stayed trapped in its slide run and could not jump out), it finally all came together. I used a picture as the concealer to hide the panel under normal circumstances.

The sequence in Figures 1-12 through 1-15 shows the final installation.

A picture hanging on the drywall.

Figure 1-12. *A picture of innocence*

| | Behind the picture, a framed opening, blocked by a wooden panel.

I open the secret compartment of the clock, and I press the secret button that lives inside it . . . |

Figure 1-13. The picture removed

| | The panel slides aside and behind it, a secret compartment is slowly revealed.

As the compartment is revealed, blue lights fade up inside it . . . to show . . . |

A presentation box containing a pair of "CTRL" and ESC" cuff links!

Figure 1-14. *Inside the secret compartment*

There, wasn't that worth all the waiting?

(well, I did warn you that I was having trouble thinking about what to put in it . . .)

Figure 1-15. *Secret compartment*

Summary

This was a great project for me, I learned a lot from doing it and had frustration and fun in pretty much equal measure.

Who knew there would turn out to be so many different ways to do it! I guess the beauty of it is that there is not a single "right" way to do it; if it works, it works–whatever method you use. It's an unusual project for an electronics book because it has as many dependencies on where you install it as on what components and parts you use.

This project was one that I have always had in the back of my mind to do. Finally, this book gave me an excuse to do it, and it did not disappoint!

However, I'm afraid I still don't know what to keep in my secret compartment.

Coming up Next

Here Kitty, Kitty: Random laser beams to drive your pets crazy.

■ ■ ■

CHAPTER 2

Project 2: Crazy Beams— Exercise Your Pet!

In this project we are going to try to give your pet (your cat or your dog) hours of harmless fun and exercise. This project is a little like the gem light project covered in Chapter 4 of *Practical AVR Microcontrollers* (Apress, 2012). This time, though, we're not out to do something ornamental; this time we have a functional aim in mind: keeping the animals entertained!

The idea for this project came from observing how much fun it can be to watch a cat or dog trying to catch the light spot cast from a presentation pointer. You've seen these things; they are very low-powered laser lights, usually no more than 5 mw and often built into a pen or a key ring. They are used to put a pinpoint of red light on a screen–usually to indicate a point or area of interest during a live presentation that uses a computer or a stills projector. A dog or a cat will happily spend a long time skittering around the floor chasing one of these light spots, while you, sitting comfortably in your chair, shine the light all around the room. The animal pounces on the light spot triumphantly. But then, the light spot escapes its grasp and it's off again. Then the light disappears altogether. Where has it gone? It's behind you! Your dog or cat can have hours of fun. The trouble is that the human wielding the pointer light usually gets tired of the game before the animal does!

So, what if there was a machine to do the light shining? One that could move the light around, casting multiple light spots, randomly speeding up and slowing down, making the light disappear and reappear again somewhere else. Endless fun! And, since a machine never gets tired, it goes on and on until the animal has had enough!

The Project

This project uses two very low power lasers attached to two servo motors. These motors allow the beams of light to be moved around in the horizontal plane. However, the laser and motor assembly are mounted on a spindle which allows them to be moved in the vertical plane by a third motor; this allows the AVR controlling the whole thing to move the beams around quite a large area.

The second laser and its associated motor are optional, you can just build the project with one laser and servo motor if you want to. Although the effect is better with two beams, the software doesn't care if any (or all) of the motors are not really there. Commodity-priced servo motors don't offer any positional sensing capability to the host computer, so unless you use far more expensive motors the Crazy Beams software has no way to sense the motor positions. This is not a problem, however; as covered in Chapter 4 of *Practical AVR Microcontrollers* (Apress, 2012), servo motors are pretty good at doing what they're told!

If you have multiple animals to entertain, you could add a third or even a fourth motor and laser. That would make lots of beams for your pets to chase. If you're scaling up the project in that way, though, you need to make sure your power supply arrangements are sufficient. The power requirements for each laser are low, but each additional servo motor adds quite a lot to the power supply load. Scaling up the project from a hardware point of view is not hard; there are lots of spare I/O pins on the AVR MCU chip and the software makes use of a motor descriptor array which can be extended.

Another way to scale up the project without extra motors and lasers would be to add prismatic diffusers, to split the beams multiple ways, although at reduced intensity. You can get some very pretty room lighting effects in this way too, but that's beyond the immediate scope of this project.

Sourcing the Lasers

Presentation pointers that incorporate low-power laser diodes are widely sold and cheap, so my first thought was to try to extract the laser diodes I needed from two of these. Having tried this, I can't recommend that approach. The problem is that those kinds of products are really not meant for disassembly: they seem to be put together as a friction fit under a lot of pressure. That means that you have to cut your way into them, making jagged edges and (in my case) deforming both the lens assembly and the laser diode in the process. My laser didn't focus properly afterward and stopped working shortly after that. So, on the whole, pillaging a presentation pointer for its laser module seems like an unexpectedly tricky job that could take a lot of tries to get right!

Fortunately, you *can* buy just the laser diode and lens assembly separately and ready wired for use with a power supply; it does cost a little more, but it's ready to go when you get it—and this is the route I eventually took.

Example products can be found at

- www.sparkfun.com/products/9906 (United States).

- www.maplin.co.uk (UK) (search for LE07).

You can also get these from various eBay vendors (search for "laser diode module"). Make sure you get +4.5V or +5V lasers, which will simplify your power supply arrangements. Don't get anything more powerful than 5 milliwatts because it will be too bright and possibly dangerous to your eyesight.

■ **Caution**   *Never* regard a laser as harmless. Using one with the recommended power level is as safe as we can make it, but *do not* ever shine the laser directly into your own eyes or anyone else's. Sight damage *will* occur. Also, make sure that the laser stays slightly unfocused when you set up your *Crazy Beams* project. This will diffuse the laser light slightly so that your pet's eyes, if they happen to look at the unit, cannot be overexposed.

The lasers I used consume about 40 ma each, which is not a lot, but about twice as much as you would want to take from an MCU pin.[1] So, we have to include our old friend the 2803 transistor array chip (see Chapter 3 of *Practical AVR Microcontrollers* [Apress, 2012]) to provide the drive that the lasers need. You could use just use NPN transistors, such as a couple of BC548s if you prefer—but by the time you've added a base resistor they'd probably take up almost the same amount of board space.

Project Build

The project consists of three major assemblies.

- A simple wooden frame.

- The horizontal motor/laser assembly

- The electronics board. You could build it on a mini-breadboard, but you could easily make a solder board version of it—it's really just two chips.

The frame has to be fairly deep, but not very long or high. So, I made this up out of some short lengths of 7" (180 mm)-wide pine plank (see Figure 2-3).

The horizontal motors frame is made from a couple of stiff plastic strips (something suitable in plastic or metal can be obtained from your usual home supplies superstore) and a couple of thick wood blocks (I used some short lengths of 2"-square table leg that I had left over from a previous project).

The horizontal assembly is mounted on a spindle so that it can swing back and forth. The spindle is made from a couple of 0.25"/M6 bolts which clear through the sides of the frame and then loosely fit into some appropriately sized threaded inserts, which screw into the side of the blocks. Figure 2-1 shows a threaded insert (see the "Secret panel" project in Chapter 1 for more details and links to where to get them).

---

[1] In fact an ATmega328 pin could sink about 40 ma, but it's an absolute maximum value which— since we would be doing it on two pins (one per laser)—is not advised.

Figure 2-1. Threaded insert

The horizontal motors are mounted on the assembly and the lasers are mounted to the top of those motors. This means that the motors can sweep the laser lights that they carry back and forth to move the light spots in the horizontal plane. Figure 2-2 shows the completed assembly with the two servo motors mounted in place but no lasers fitted yet; you can see a threaded insert at the end of the assembly. There is no "right" size for this assembly because the size depends on some variable factors:

- Whether you are going to use two horizontal motors and lasers (as per the picture) or just one.

- How far apart you want the traveling light spots to be. If you have several pets to amuse, it may be that you want greater separation, in which case the motors will need to be mounted wider apart to increase the distance. You may also want space for scaling if you have more additional pets to amuse and want to add more horizontal beams.

- The maximum rotation of your servo motors—as covered in Chapter 4 of *Practical AVR Microcontrollers* (Apress, 2012) there is actually some quite surprising variation in this supposedly "standard" factor.

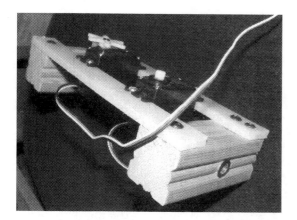

Figure 2-2. *Completed horizontal assembly*

Obviously, a little servo motor pushing and pulling is going to have a much easier job if the horizontal assembly swings freely. It's therefore pretty important that you make sure to place the threaded inserts as centrally in the end blocks as you can get them.

When you put all this together you should have a free-swinging assembly that the vertical motor (via the linkage mentioned earlier) can easily move to and fro, under control of the MCU. Don't over tighten the bolts through the threaded inserts, and make sure the clearance holes through the frame sides are just large enough to allow the bolt to rotate freely.

The vertical motor is built onto the frame, raised up by appropriately sized wooden blocks–as shown in Figure 2-3. The motor needs to sit at a height where, via a linkage made with stiff wire bent into shape, it can push and pull the horizontal assembly back and forth, affecting the vertical position of the laser spots. It doesn't have to provide a large amount of movement, since a small change in the angle of the lasers makes quite a big difference to the beam's position. The software on the prototype only needs to move the vertical motor over about 30% of its possible travel, and this makes a perfectly adequate difference to the beam positions.

Figure 2-3. *Crazy Beams project frame (vertical servo motor in place)*

29

You could, if you wanted to make the project "disappear" better, paint the frame in black or some other darker color. I left mine white, since it lives in my office/workshop area so appearance is not a big issue.

Assembly

Before you begin assembly it's a good idea to make sure that each servo motor you plan to use is reset to its zero degrees position. This is essential for getting the laser mounting right and for getting the wire link set up correctly.

I've found that some motors reset to their zero position as soon as you connect their voltage pins (almost always black and red wires) to a +5V source, but leave their servo lead (usually either white or yellow) disconnected. Some motors don't reset, though, and for these you should use the servo motor reset program (you can also download this program from the book's web site (www.apress.com/9781430244462). To use this, you'll have to jump ahead a bit to the circuit diagram in Figure 2-7 and Figure 2-8 and connect your motors up as shown there.

The servo reset program is very simple, as follows:

```
/*
 Servo Motor Reset Program:
 Reset all listed servo motors to zero degrees
 */
#include <Servo.h>
#define HORIZ01_PIN 6
#define HORIZ02_PIN 9
#define VERT01_PIN 10

Servo horiz01;
Servo horiz02;
Servo vert01;

void setup()
{
  Serial.begin(9600);
  Serial.println("Resetting motors");
  horiz01.attach(HORIZ01_PIN );
  horiz02.attach(HORIZ02_PIN );
  vert01.attach(VERT01_PIN);

  horiz01.write(0);
  horiz02.write(0);
  vert01.write(0);
  Serial.println("Reset done");
}
```

```
void loop()
{
  // Main loop left intentionally empty!
}
```

This servo reset program just uses the servo library (see Chapter 4 of *Practical AVR Microcontrollers* [Apress, 2012] for details) to set each motor to zero degrees; it uses only the setup() function, and the loop() is empty. When you upload and run the program, you may find that nothing appears to happen. This could mean you have not wired up the motors correctly, but more likely it means that the motors are already at their zero degrees position. To be sure, try temporarily changing the

```
"...write(0)"
```

lines to something like

```
"...write(100)"
```

and try again. That should make some movement, if your wiring is right. Don't forget to change the code back to zero and run it again to make sure your motor is reset to zero degrees before you install it. The main program for this project also includes numerous features that can be useful during setup and alignment of the mechanical elements. See the section "Crazy Beams Software Code Walk."

It's *important* that you make a note of which way your motor turns when it goes from angle 0 to angle 100. You'll need this information to better visualize positioning the laser diodes and setting the linkage from the horizontal assembly to the vertical motor.

Once the motors are reset you can begin mounting the laser modules on the servo motors. I used the longest and widest of the horns (the plastic wheels and fittings that usually come with the motor are the "horns") and some 22 SWG[2] (0.7 mm) tinned wire to bind the lasers to it. You can use various kinds of wire for this purpose–piano wire or garden wire might be suitable. Any metal wire in the range 20 SWG to 25 SWG should work well.

You need to bind the laser to one side of the center so that you can still access the center screw on the horn to tighten it up. The photo in Figure 2-4 shows how this looks when it's done. Twist the wire up tight with a pair of pliers. Make it tight enough to hold the laser very securely, but don't go crazy. The wire will snap or the laser casing might deform. The wire actually does hold the lasers very securely; however, when the setup alignment is done, you can put a dab of glue between the plastic horn and the laser module to make extra sure it stays in place—but don't do that before you have aligned the laser.

---

[2]SWG = Standard Wire Gauge.

Figure 2-4. *Laser diode mounted on servo motor*

The next job is to install the linkage from the vertical motor to the horizontal assembly. Mount it so that, with the vertical motor at its reset position, the horizontal assembly is held such that the laser light will just shine *inside* the frame. This gives the software the ability to reset the beams so that they don't leave the frame. The linkage from the vertical motor to the horizontal assembly is made of a dual strand of 22 SWG (0.7 mm) tinned steel wire—again, you can use anything comparable. As long as your horizontal assembly swings freely this linkage should be plenty strong enough. You'll need a small hole through the lower plastic crossbar so that the linkage has a good anchor. As before, the vertical motor is fitted with the longest of the plastic horns it came with (this maximizes the swing the motor can exert).

Figure 2-5 shows the linkage in place, in this photo the motor is set at about 70 degrees of travel; when it's set to less, the motor will turn counter clockwise and pull the assembly back toward us, lowering the vertical setting.

Figure 2-5. *Vertical motor to horizontal frame linkage (see also Figure 2-6)*

Figure 2-6 shows the overall assembly.

Figure 2-6. *Overall view of the Crazy Beams project*

As long as you have made sure the motors are all reset to their zero degrees position, aligning the lasers is quite straightforward. You just need to put the horn on the motor such that the laser will point to a base position when at its "at rest" position. We can handle the rest of the positioning issues in the software (see "Crazy Beams Code Walk" section – below).

The Electronics

The diagram in Figure 2-7 shows the electronics for this project. This diagram is broadly the same however you elect to build the electronic side of the project (breadboard, solder board etc).

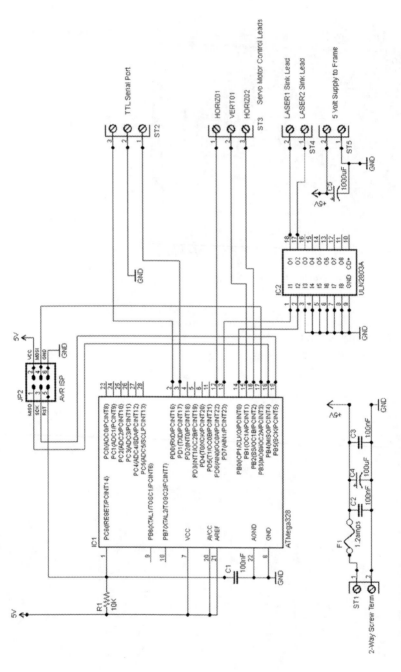

Figure 2-7. Crazy Beams main circuit diagram

Note that because we are using motors, a fuse is a must-have: you need one somewhere in the + lead of the power supply.

We are again using a trusty ATmega328 chip. We are using it in its internal 8 MHz clock mode (see Chapter 3 of *Practical AVR Microcontrollers* [Apress, 2012] for details on using AVRDude to set up this mode of operation) which is plenty fast enough for this application. In addition (as previously mentioned), we need a ULN2803A driver transistor array,

Table 2-1 shows the AVR pins we use here.

Table 2-1. *AVR Pins Usage*

AVR Pin Number	Arduino Name	Usage
2	RXD	Receive data
3	TXD	Transmit data
12	Digital pin 6	Horizontal Motor 1 Servo Control Line
13	Digital pin 7	Laser1 (HIGH = ON)
14	Digital pin 8	Laser2 (HIGH = ON)
15	Digital pin 9	Horizontal Motor 2 Servo Control Line
16	Digital pin 10	Vertical Motor 1 Servo Controller Line

As previously discussed, this leaves lots of spare I/O pins free for adding more beams and motors.

Because they are electromechanical devices, even the comparatively well-behaved servo motors can be quite brutal to a power supply (as compared to purely electronic devices). Therefore, we add a couple of 1000 uF capacitors to the circuit in this project to better protect the logic circuits against power supply dips and spikes. C5 goes onto the main electronics circuit board (test rig) and the other, C6, goes inside the crazy beams frame box. One effect of adding this extra capacitance is that the rise time of the power supply will increase; that is, the time it takes at switch on for the PSU to reach +5V from nothing will be increased. This can cause problems with AVR reset. So if, after you add the capacitors, your AVR never (or sometimes doesn't) starts up, you may need to increase the value of C1 (e.g., to 0.47 uF) to make the power-on reset pulse at the AVR's pin 1 a little longer. That should solve the problem, if it occurs.

The power arrangement shown in the circuit diagram assumes that everything runs off +5 volts, which it probably will. Most small servo motors run on +5 volts as do the specified laser diodes. However, if you somehow end up needing a +12V supply as well, just reuse the power supply design from the sliding panel project from Chapter 1, which will do the job nicely.

As you can see, the connections to the crazy beams frame come off the board via seven screw connector terminals (not including the TTL level serial port, which you can optionally use for this project as you'll see when we get to the software description). Unless you're building a custom board that can live inside the frame, you'll need to make up a seven-way wiring harness to convey the signals from the board to the frame. You'll see in the photos how I did this; I just used a miniature plastic screw terminal inside the box.

The diagram in Figure 2-8 shows the wiring inside the project's wood frame. The essential connections are as follows:

- +5V to the + lead of each motor, and also to the positive side (red wire) of the two laser diodes.

- Ground connects to each motor (note: C6 doing the smoothing function described above).

- Each motor's servo lead is brought back to the board individually.

- The negative lead of each of the laser diodes is brought back individually to the board.

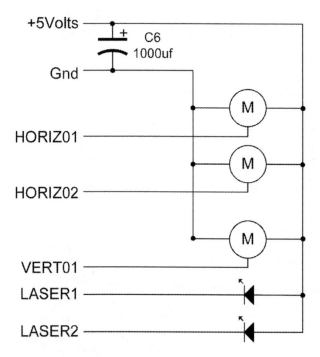

Figure 2-8. *Motors and laser wiring*

It's tempting to want to make the wiring run between the electronics and the frame as long as possible, but although I haven't tried it, I think that you might start to run into noise problems if the wires were more than about 18 inches.

That concludes the description of the physical aspects of the project. Let's now move on to the software.

Crazy Beams—The Software

The software for the Crazy Beams project is currently version 3. I did two previous versions (how did you guess!) but scrapped them due to various defects and shortcomings.

The final version uses a data structure (servoMotorDetails) to describe the properties and current state of each motor. An array instance of this data structure, motors, holds the descriptions of the servo motors and their state (see next section "Software–Positioning Parameters and Timing Constants," for more details). Various functions within the program play around with the contents of this array, and then they call setMotorAngles(), which is the only function in the main part of the program that writes to the hardware.

The main two components of the loop() function are to generate a random number which, based on the number generated, can change the pathways of the crazy beams in some random way. We'll see details of this in the section "Crazy Beams Software Code Walk." The other component of the main loop is just to progress the "animation" of the laser beams. They basically scan back and forth and a little bit up and down—which would get boring after a while, but the random number handler's actions break it all up and make the beams suddenly do something different. There is no predictable pattern to the pathway of the beams—they are, literally, crazy! Also within the main loop we check to see if any single letter commands have come in from the serial channel.

Software—Positioning Parameters and Timing Constants

Just before we take a code walk, it might be helpful to explain in a little more detail the function of the constants and values declared at the start of the Crazy Beams software.

In this project, we don't use the full rotation of the servo motors; we only need to use a part of each motor's rotational range to get the effects we want. However, that range will vary from build to build, affected by mounting arrangements, distances between motors and frame, and beam length. So, each motor has the following parameters associated with it. These are stored (along with some other items that add to the description of each of the three motors) in an array of C-structs called motors, which is of type servoMotorDetails.

- restAngle: This is the angle the motor will be set to when the project is not in use, or during initial reset.

- startAngle: This is the "home" position for the motor; it is the start point of its useful rotational range within this project.

- endAngle: This is the maximum rotation we need the motor to do within the context of this project. If the motor rotates further than this, then the laser (or mechanical linkage it controls) may hit something, or a beam may shine somewhere we don't want it to. The software will never send the motor beyond this point.

- maxAngle: This is the maximum angle to which the motor is capable of turning. It is never used by this software.

- currentAngle: This is the angle to which the motor is currently turned.

Two timing constants control the beam travel speeds: LOOP_DELAY_MIN and LOOP_DELAY_MAX. In the main loop, after each beam move, the program delays for a few milliseconds. One of the randomly chosen actions in the main loop is to change this timing value to a random value in order to make the beams move faster or slower. These two constants constrain the randomly chosen timing value to a range that makes sense for this application.

Crazy Beams Software Code Walk

The Arduino code for Crazy Beams is downloadable from the book's web site (www.apress.com/9781430244462). The code walk shown in Table 2-2 explains all the functions within the program.

Table 2-2. *Crazy Beams Software—Functions List*

Function	Commentary
Declarations Header Section (args: none)	In this initial section, the Arduino pin numbers for the motors and the lasers are defined and various constants are declared. This section also includes the servo library, which is what we use to provide the PWM values needed by the motors.
	The servoMotorDetails struct is declared, and the motors array filled with a mixture of constants, initial values, and references to instances of servo motors. Note that mtrsArrayTop needs to be declared here because, in Arduino's environment, there is no easy way for software to dynamically discover the upper bound of an array. This tells the rest of the program the highest index number of the motors array.
setup() args: None	The setup() function attaches the relevant pin numbers to the servo motor object instances. It then sets the motors to their rest position, then to their end positions, back to the rest position, and then finally to their start positions. This is intended to ensure a full mechanical reset and to ensure there are no blockages to movement over the full required movement range. Essentially, the theory is that users get used to how a machine resets, and if anything sounds different than usual they will investigate it before too much damage is done. Nice theory!
	Next, the laser pins are initialized and the lasers flash quickly four times to show they are okay.
	Finally the version message is sent out to the serial channel. Usage of the serial channel in this project is optional. However, having a TTL level serial USB dongle on a laptop or desktop does give you extra control over the unit. See Chapter 2 of *Practical AVR Microcontrollers* (Apress, 2012) for more detail on USB serial dongles.

(continued)

Table 2-2. (*continued*)

Function	Commentary
`loop()` args: None	As previously described, the main loop of this program progresses movement of the horizontal beam motors and the vertical motor in a nice smooth fashion; each one will scan from its start position to its end position and back again, over and over. The code to do this is located near the end of the `loop()` function. However, in order to get to that, the processor has to get through a number of preliminaries.

- First, the program checks to see if any characters have been sent in from the serial channel. If characters have been received, then the `processKbInput()` function (described below) is called to handle them.

- Next, the value of the doNothing Boolean is checked. If this is found to be true, then the `loop()` is exited. As the name of this Boolean implies, this is the mechanism whereby the unit is disabled. The value of doNothing is toggled by receiving an "S" command from the serial channel (see description of `processKbInput()`).

Next, we generate a random number. In the program as-supplied, this random number will be between 0 and 199. Most of the numbers in the range don't have any effect. However, within the main loop there is a list (in a switch-case set) of numbers that do cause changes to the beam paths to be made. Note that the beam path changes are made by changing items in the motors array, *not* by directly writing to the hardware. The contents of the array are used to write out positioning commands to the hardware, only at the very end of `loop()`.

The random number matches do the following things:

- Set the horizontal beam positioning motors to a random position (somewhere between its start and end position).

- Set the vertical beam positioning motor to a random position (somewhere between its start and end positions).

- Turn beams off and disable movement (by setting the selfDisabled Boolean).

- Turn beams back on and re-enable movement (by clearing the selfDisabled Boolean).

- Change the speed of operations by changing the delay value in the main loop. This changes the speed at which the beams will move around.

(*continued*)

Table 2-2. (*continued*)

Function	Commentary
	The effect of injecting this randomness is that the beams will move around smoothly for a while and then suddenly change course or speed. Then they disappear and shortly afterward they reappear somewhere else. If you want less randomness, just increase the higher value in random(0,200) from 200 to a larger number. This makes it less likely that any of the defined numbers will come up in a random selection. Decrease it (no lower than 10 though) if you want even more randomness.
	Finally, we call the functions to progress the horizontal and vertical motion, and it is these that actually call the setMotorAngles() function, which positions the hardware according to the contents of the motors array.
motorsHome() motorsRest() motorsToMax() motorsToEnd() motorsToStart() Args: None Return values: None	These functions all do similar things. They position each of the motors to a known position, such as its rest position or its end position. These were described in the previous section of the text. None of these functions take any arguments, or (since there is no sensory feedback from the servo motors used) return any values.
turnOnLasers() turnOffLasers() args: None. Return values: None	These functions turn both lasers on or off. They take no arguments and return no values.

(*continued*)

Table 2-2. (*continued*)

Function	Commentary
progressHorizMotion() progressVerticalMotion() args: None. Return values: None	These functions progress the motion of the horizontal and vertical motors. They manipulate the contents of the members of the motors array that relate to the horizontal motors. For each horizontal motor the following processing is performed: • If the movingForward member is true then the currentAngle member of the array is incremented. If it becomes more than the value indicated in maxAngle then the end of travel in the current direction has been reached and the currentAngle is decremented again, and the movingForward flag for this motor is set to false. • If the movingForward member is false, then the currentAngle member of the array is decremented. If that makes it less than startAngle, then the motor has moved as far in the reverse direction as it can and movingForward is set to true. At the end of this processing, the motor position has been moved on by one step, and a reversal of direction made, if needed. Finally, the motor values are written out to the hardware using setMotorAngles()
horizontalMotorRandom() verticalMotorRandom() args: None Return values: None	These functions set the currentAngle member of each motor's entry in the motors array to a random value. The random value will be somewhere between the motor's startAngle and endAngle values.
setMotorAngles() args: int motorID	This function sets the angle of one or more motors, as defined in the motors array. It takes one argument, motorID, which is an integer that defines which member of the motors array is to be used. However, if motorID is sent as -1, then *all* motors are set. The currentAngle values held in motors are assumed to be in range and valid. This is the only point in the program where the motor positions are directly set from the software. All other functions that want to set the motor positions modify values in the motors array and then call this function.
lasersOn() lasersOff() args: None Return values: None	These functions turn both lasers on or off.

(*continued*)

Table 2-2. (*continued*)

Function	Commentary
changeLoopDelay() args: None return Value: None	This function changes the global variable loopDelay to a random value between LOOP_DELAY_MIN and LOOP_DELAY_MAX. As mentioned previously, this has the effect of changing the beam progress speed by changing the time delay in the programs main loop.
processKbInput() args: None Return value: None	This function is called from the main loop when it recognizes that something has been received from the serial channel. This gives a way for a user (using a TTL serial port on another computer) to exercise control over the Crazy Beams unit, and to see the message stream coming out of the unit. This function implements a number of single-character commands. Commands are not echoed and can be lowercase or uppercase, either will work. The commands are as follows: • "S" = Toggles the state of the doNothing Boolean flag. When set, this flag sets the unit into inert mode. The lasers are turned off and all automated movement ceases. • "L" = Toggles the state of the lasers. If they were on, they go off and vice versa. This is almost useless unless the unit is inert, since the laser state is regularly changed during normal operations. However, when the unit is inert it is a very useful guide to checking laser positions and focus. • "1" and "2" = These comments cause only a single laser to remain on, for example "1" will put laser 1 on, but 2 will go off. Again, this is only useful when the unit is inert. • "E" = Makes all motors go to their end position. Used in inert mode for checking motor limits. • "S" = Makes all motors go to their start position. Used in inert mode for checking motor limits. • "R" = Makes all motors go to their rest positions.

> ▓ **Note** There is no M command for setting motors to their max position, since often this can cause mechanical damage or impact.

• Any other command results in an error message listing the available commands.

So, that concludes our code walk for Crazy Beams, and indeed the project description.

Summary

This chapter has detailed the design, mechanical construction, electronics, and software of a Crazy Beams project. This is a project that is intended to provide unending entertainment for your pets, by giving them beams of light moving around the floor that they can chase, but never catch! If you are building the project you should take due note of the safety messages in the text around laser usage and fusing. The project is readily adaptable to a variety of configurations, either less or more complex (e.g., depending on the number of pets you have to entertain).

Coming Up Next

WordDune; a game of words.

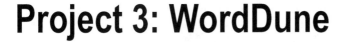

CHAPTER 3

Project 3: WordDune

How Much Do You *Really* See?

This project is all about looking good! That is, looking and doing it well.

The quickness of the computer often deceives the eye. We're all quite used to thinking that we see moving images on a computer or TV screen when what we really see is very fast image manipulation and animation. In this project we use an LCD display to improve your looking skills.

The human brain is very good at pattern recognition; we can pick out a single familiar face in a crowd of hundreds of people, we can see pictures in apparently random clouds in the sky or in the flames of a fire, we can pick out somebody saying our name across a noisy room. Although we *all* have this ability to see order in apparent chaos, we have it in different degrees. How good are you? This game tests your ability to pick out complete words from a veritable dune of numbers, letters, and symbols. It's a really easy game–at first: but at each level it gets more and more difficult . . . see where you reach your limit!

WordDune is a game in which actual words or phrases are semihidden in an on-screen torrent of random characters and letters. The torrent gets faster and denser at each level of the game. Your task is to spot four words which repeatedly hide among the ever-changing random characters. At the end of each level, you have to be able to say what the four words were.

The Hardware

Aside from the ATmega328 AVR chip, the only additional hardware for this game is a four-line LCD display and a push button. This makes this an easy project to build on the breadboard; if you want a permanent version of it, you could build it on a tripad or a strip board.

This project uses a 4x20 (4 rows by 20 columns) LCD display built around the Hitachi HD44780 LCD controller.

Example products might include the following:

- Sparkfun SKU: LCD-00256 (United States).

- Maplin Stock Number: N30AZ (UK).

- Various online auction site vendors.

I strongly recommend you solder a row of header pins to the display so that it can plug into a breadboard. Later on, if you ever decide to make a permanent version of this project you could use a socket header strip on your permanent board in which to plug in the display.

Figure 3-1. *Header pin and socket strips*

Suitable example products for header pins are

- Sparkfun SKU: PRT-10158 and PRT-10007 (United States).

- Maplin Stock Number: JW59P.

- The header sockets, which are usually available from various eBay vendors.

You can connect to the display by using just the lower four bits of the interface to save some MCU I/O pins and because it's fast enough for our purposes here. I use the LiquidCrystal library–bundled with Arduino–to do the detailed display driving.

There are two ways to update the game's dictionary (see section "WordDune Gameplay").

- You can simply modify the word set that's included in the code and reprogram the microcontroller–using the ISP connection.

- You can use a TTL level serial interface to use the game's embedded command set to remove and add items. We'll look at the command set in the section "WordDune Commands."

Figure 3-2 shows the circuit diagram for the game.

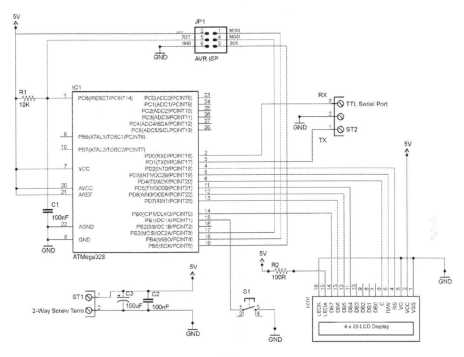

Figure 3-2. *WordDune Hardware Circuit Diagram*

As you can see, the WordDune hardware is pretty straightforward. The ATmega328 MCU is, as ever, center stage and is running without an external crystal, since an 8 MHz clock speed is plenty fast enough for this project. See Chapter 3 of *Practical AVR Microcontrollers* (Apress, 2012) for details on setting the MCU's clock rate, if it's not already done.

There is an ISP Jack that allows you to update the software AND the word list from your main computer. This is pretty important in this project, so whatever way you decide to build the project (strip board or breadboard) you will need this. We covered building a thing called "The test bed" breadboard in Chapter 2 of *Practical AVR Microcontrollers* (Apress, 2012). That section showed how to implement an ISP jack on a breadboard, using a ribbon cable to breadboard adaptor from Sparkfun.

There are two other screw terminal connectors shown. The first brings power (just +5V and ground needed): If you're building a permanent version of this game, you might want to make ST1 (screw terminal 1) a panel-mounted female DC power socket instead: this would have to be a physical match for the plug of whatever you use as your power source (see the Wikipedia article 'Coaxial Power Connector' for details about DC power plugs and sockets). You could use various kinds of +5V supply, such as

- An external +5V mains supply (a so-called wall wart) capable of supplying 500 milliamps or more.

- A USB to DC power lead. This project uses only about 350 ma, so a USB port from most desktop machines can supply this, as can devices like a mains to USB power supply, or a "charge mule" (a mains charger that has its own internal battery that you can later use to charge your USB kit if you are away from a mains outlet).

- A set of three AA batteries (alkaline preferred), supplying about 4.5 volts. You would be well advised to check with the vendor of your display before committing to battery operation, however; some (but not all) LCD displays I have tried lose brightness and contrast very quickly when operated even slightly below +5V. If you are not running on +5V you could replace resistor R2 with a slightly lower value. However, you need to refer to the data sheet of the LCD display that you buy to determine a new value for a different voltage. Make certain that you don't take the backlight LED over its maximum current, or else you will damage it. The data sheets for some LCD displays are strangely silent on the subject of maximum backlight LED current. If in doubt, 50 ma is a reasonably safe guess.

The capacitors C2 and C3 are to smooth out any fluctuations in the power supply.

The TTL level serial port (ST2) allows you connect to an external terminal emulator running in your desktop machine. Your breadboard probably already has this of course, but if not, or if you are building a keeper version of this game, take a look at the "Serial ports" discussion near the end of Chapter 3 of *Practical AVR Microcontrollers* (Apress, 2012) to see how to easily setup a serial channel to a desktop or laptop using a USB to TTL serial dongle.

The press button (momentary action, single pole, push to make) switch can be any switch that suits. In this application I'd advise a nice "clicky" switch that gives you strong feedback when you press it: you press the button a lot during this game, so you need something that you can be sure you have pressed. If you're not keen on having the push-button switch mounted on the breadboard, or it doesn't have the right connector type to plug in, you can put long leads on the switch and mount it in a small plastic box (you may find something suitable going out for recycling).

WordDune: The Build

I initially built WordDune on a breadboard. I started by installing the 4x20 LCD display (with header pins fitted) onto the breadboard on the upper side at column 40. Then, I installed tie-high and tie-low jumpers as indicated on the circuit diagram; I also installed R2. Figure 3-3 shows this stage.

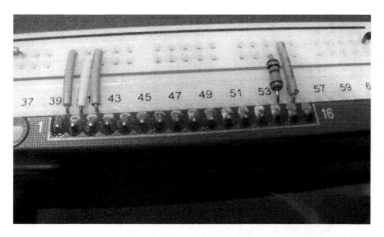

Figure 3-3. *WordDune: LCD display at column 40 with ties and R2 installed*

Next, I installed the seven "flying" jumpers that are required to link the signals between the MCU and the display. The photo in Figure 3-4 depicts this step.

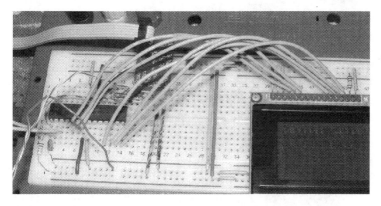

Figure 3-4. *WordDune flying jumpers installed*

The next step was to connect a push button S1 between ground and AVR pin 15 (see Figure 3-5). I took a button switch and soldered some wires to it (I had cut the wires out of an old CAT5 network cable). I've found that solid (not stranded) wires pulled out of old CAT5 cables make ideal connections because the stripped wire ends fit neatly into breadboard holes (see Figure 3-6).

Figure 3-5. *WordDune: The push button*

Figure 3-6. *Push button wired to the breadboard*

The push button I used in fact has an LED indicator in it. I haven't used that in this version, but a spare pin on the AVR could easily be used to make the button light up to indicate times when the program is waiting for the button to be pressed. I leave this as an exercise for any reader who would like to take this extra step.

While doing the extensive testing for the game (it's a tough job, but somebody had to do it) I did in fact get tired of the push button flopping around, so I liberated a coffee jar lid from our recycling box, cut a button-size hole in the top of it, cut a wire-size hole in the side, spray painted the whole thing black, and mounted the button into it (see Figure 3-7). Hey, presto! A much more usable button mount, All except it doesn't any more. Who who photo-suited Nescafe out of this photo? It's okay, I don't care, just a surprise! (see Figure 3-8).

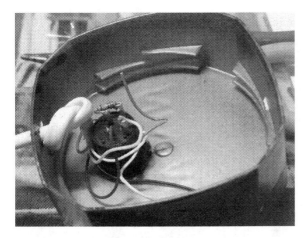

Figure 3-7. *The coffee jar lid button mount*

Figure 3-8. *Button holder complete*

So, for building the game on the breadboard, that's about all there is to it!

WordDune Gameplay

A WordDune is a random jumble of numbers letter and symbols in which a set of four actual words is hidden, somewhere. The trouble is, this dune keeps shifting; the words appear but they are soon buried in the continuing onscreen torrent of random characters and letters. The torrent gets faster and denser at each level. You, as the player must spot the words. At the end of a level, you have to know what the four words were.

For each level, four words are randomly chosen from a list of words. You can add or remove words from this list to keep the game fresh. Each word is on screen at a random place for a few moments, four times during each level. However, as the levels progress, the onscreen time of each word gets less, and the clutter around the actual words gets denser, making it harder to spot.

The challenge is to identify the four words and–if you're playing against others–to say them out loud before the four words are revealed at the end of the round. You can play the game in a group, or just on your own as a personal challenge.

The game has two distinct splash sequences (animated sequences that play over and over while the software is waiting for someone to start off a WordDune game). The screenshots in Figures 3-9 through 3-15 show the game in progress at various levels.

Figure 3-9. *WordDune: Start prompt*

Figure 3-10. *WordDune: Level 0 in progress*

The first two screenshots show the start prompt that immediately follows the animated attractor sequence, and a game in progress at level 0. In level 0 words appear on the screen and are only gradually erased by spaces. It's so easy you could do it in your sleep!

When a game level ends you get a screen like the one shown in Figure 3-11. When you click, you get shown the four words that you were searching for in the level that just completed. Then, it's onto the next and slightly harder level. Figure 3-12 illustrates the Level 1 introducer screen.

Figure 3-11. *WordDune: End of level 0 screen*

Figure 3-12. *Level 1: The introducer screen*

Figure 3-13. *WordDune: CLIFF in lowercase soup*

Figure 3-14. *WordDune: Level 3, Albatross disappearing*

As the levels progress, it gets harder to see the words, which are, first, among lowercase random letters and then later among random letters and numbers. And the words start getting overwritten faster and faster with each new level. In Figures 3-13 and 3-14, CLIFF is quite easy to spot and you can probably just about see where ALBATROSS was, but a short time ago!

So, it starts very easy, but gets harder and harder. On the easy levels it's worth remembering that, once you've spotted the four words, you can terminate a level early by clicking the button (see Figure 3-15).

Figure 3-15. *WordDune: The game end*

53

WordDune: Game Software Setup

When you have the hardware ready (as per the circuit diagram in Figure 3- 1 and the build instructions) you can install the software. The installation of this software is a little unusual.

▓ **Note** You can download the sketch for this example at www.apress.com/9781430244462.

Setting up the game proceeds in two steps.

- You first open the WordDune sketch and compile and upload it into the AVR using the usual upload method within the Arduino IDE. This, as usual, performs a chip erase before uploading (which, of course, erases the EEPROM as well as all the flash memory).

- Next, you use AVRDude to put the contents of the file WordDune_EEPROM.Hex into the AVR's EEPROM memory. In WordDune, the EEPROM is used to hold a catalog of prompts and error messages: but the main use for it is to hold a dictionary of words that the game will use. As we shall see in the "WordDune Commands" section later on, you can add words, delete words, and list the contents of this dictionary using commands into the serial channel.

The idea of setting up the software in this way is to maximize the available space in EEPROM for the word list (which for, some reason, I misleadingly called a dictionary). The game works best when you have a large list of words. By adding new words you build up the size of the list; you can typically get about 90 words of average length into the space available in an ATmega328 EEPROM space. All words are entered and held in uppercase. If you try to enter a word that's already in the list it will be rejected as a duplicate. The maximum length of a word is 20 characters. You start off with a default set of ten words, but you can add to or take away words and list all the current words using commands into the serial port.

The EEPROM also holds the error messages catalog and the help text that reminds you of what commands are available (see section "WordDune Commands"). We could hold all this stuff in flash memory (using PROGMEM) or we could use the unsupported EEMEM keyword in the code to specify EEPROM contents, but it's easier (and uses completely supported Arduino functions) to do it this way.

Here is the detailed procedure for installing the game, once you have constructed the hardware. You will need the WordDune.PDE file containing the Word_Dune V3 sketch. You will need the WordDune_EEPROM.Hex file (which actually contains just raw bytes, not a hex dump). You will need to use AVRDude to upload the contents of the hex file into the AVR's EEPROM.

First, you load up Word_Dune_V3 (see Figure 3-16) into Arduino. Press the "Upload" button to build (compile) the program and upload it into your AVR. The program itself should be approximately 15 KB in size.

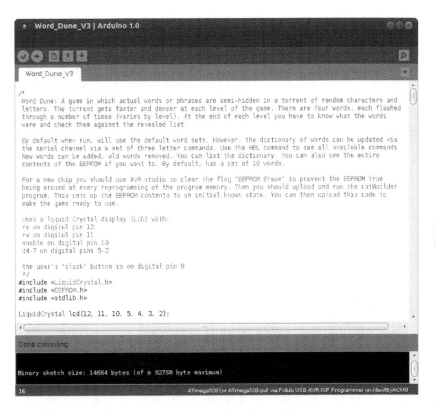

Figure 3-16. *WordDune: Word_Dune_V3 sketch in Arduino*

Now, start up a terminal window and execute the following AVRDude command:

```
avrdude -p m328 -P /dev/ttyACM0 -c avrisp2 -U eeprom:w:WordDune_EEPROM.Hex:r
```

You'll need to adapt this command if you are using some other variant of AVR (e.g., an ATmega328p) and you'll almost certainly need to change the /dev/ttyACM0 port name to whatever one you are using for your AVR programmer. For example, on a Windows system, you would use a COM port number such as COM2 instead. The section "AVRDude" in Chapter 3 of *Practical AVR Microcontrollers* (Apress, 2012) contains help on finding out your port number if you need it. That book's Chapter 3 also contains help in other related areas regarding using AVRDude level MCU programming.

Once the EEPROM upload is complete (WordDune will restart after the upload because the chip is reset as the last part of that upload) you're ready to start playing–as per the earlier game instructions.

WordDune Commands

WordDune supports a number of commands that you can issue via the TTL serial channel. When you are typing these commands, you will sometimes experience a second or so delay before the characters are echoed back; this is because the AVR is doing things on the LCD screen that delay the response. Nothing is lost; it's just a very short delay in echoing the characters you type.

In summary,

- All commands and words are in UPPERCASE.

- You only need the first three characters of the command for it to be recognized, but you can type in the whole command if you want to (e.g., DIC or DICTIONARY will both work).

- If you make a mistake, you can use the backspace key on your keyboard to rub out characters.

- Pressing CTRL/R will show you what characters you have typed in your command so far.

- Press the return or Enter key when your command is complete.

The following table provides a list and description of each of the commands:

Command	Description
HELP	Shows a list of all the available commands
ADD [Word]	Add a new word to the dictionary. All words will be uppercase. If word is already in the dictionary (the word list) then it will be rejected as a duplicate. If word was added, confirmation is given. The number of free characters remaining in the word list, after this word has been added, is also shown. Example: "ADD SPINNING."
DEPROM	Show a hex dump of the entire EEPROM: shows a hex dump (hex values plus actual characters) of the EEPROM contents. This is mainly a debug feature.
DICTIONARY	Show a list of the words in the dictionary. Gives a numbered list of the currently known words.
SWC	Show Word Count–shows how many words are in the dictionary (word list).
LEVEL [LevelID #]	If used alone, just shows the current game level number. If used with an argument, sets the game level to the indicated value. Game levels number from 0 (beginner) to 6 (Impossible!) Example: "LEV 2"
DELETE [Word]	Delete the indicated word. Example: "DEL SPINNING."

General Software Structure

The WordDune software comprises four blocks of data:

- The main body of code for the game. This is, as usual, stored in the flash program memory.

- A catalog of messages and prompts that the program uses to interact with and inform the user, both on the LCD screen and also via the serial channel, if active. This message catalog approach is useful because

  - If messages are simply included in the main code (i.e., they just occur inline in the code in various `println()` function), then the strings of text comprising those messages have to be stored in the main flash memory. In the WordDune case it's not a problem, since there is plenty of spare code space when using an ATmega328. However, where the program code body is larger, and there are more than a few messages, this can soon eat up all your code memory to the point where your software no longer fits.

    You might think that you could declare the messages as static variables. However, it turns out that is an even worse alternative, since static values are held first in flash memory (as part of the program) but then they *also* get cached at runtime in RAM memory, which is a scarce resource on an AVR chip.

  - Having the program's messages in a catalog makes it easier to change the language the program "speaks." If you wanted to change all the program's messages to, for example, German, it would be quite easy to do, since most are in one place and not distributed throughout the code.

- The help text, which is put out to the serial port in response to a HELP command. Again this is, in MCU terms, quite a lot of data.

- The word list (called the dictionary in the software for reasons that now escape me). Although the code includes an initial set of ten words, the idea is that you will add a lot more words via serial channel commands once you have the game working.

In the WordDune implementation, the message catalog, the help text, and the word list are all held in the MCU's EEPROM. As you will remember, this is nonvolatile but reprogrammable memory on the AVR chip which is available to store user data.

In the game setup instructions we installed a ready-made EEPROM image using AVRDude (see "Game Software Setup"). This image was actually built by another Arduino sketch called CatBuilder (available from this book's web site, www.apress.com/9781430244462). This sketch programs the EEPROM memory from a set of text arrays. If you wanted to make alterations to the message catalog, this is where you should do it. The steps are as follows:

- Make your alterations to the data sections of CatBuilder and resave the sketch.

- Compile and upload your modified version of CatBuilder into your MCU.

- Let the modified CatBuilder run.

- Once it completes, use AVRDude to save your new EEPROM image into a new file with a descriptive name, something like

  ```
  avrdude -p m328 -P /dev/ttyACM0 -c avrisp2 -U
  eeprom:r:WordDune_German.Hex:r
  ```

  (Again, you will need to adjust the port name from /dev/ttyACM0 to whatever you are using, and perhaps use a different AVR part code if you're not using an ATmega328).

From the perspective of an Arduino sketch, the EEPROM is seen as a set of read-writable bytes, numbering from 0-n (where n is the last byte). These are accessed as follows:

```
EEPROM.read(x) ;   // Returns a byte value from EEPROM address x.
EEPROM.write(x,y); // Writes the byte value y into EEPROM address x.
```

CatBuilder fills the EEPROM space with a set of three catalog data structures, the message catalog, the help message catalog, and the dictionary (word list) catalog. The first six bytes of EEPROM contain pointers to the start address of each of these catalogs. Each pointer is a 16-bit value, stored in two bytes. Specifically, these are as follows:

> EEPROM Bytes 0&1 = EEPROM address of the message catalogue (low byte first).

> EEPROM Bytes 2&3 = EEPROM address of the help message catalogue (low byte first).

> EEPROM Bytes 4&5 = EEPROM address of the start of the dictionary (low byte first).

The format of these catalogs is very simple. They use seven-bit ASCII characters. ASCII stands for American Standard Code for Information Interchange: a standardized Western alphabet and number coding scheme. See Arduino's help page on ASCII in the reference section or on the Wikipedia page

http://en.wikipedia.org/wiki/ASCII

Each catalog entry is a series of ASCII coded seven-bit characters, with the final character having bit 7 set, to indicate the end of the catalog entry. A byte containing 255 at what should be the start of an entry indicates the end of the catalog. The following table illustrates this arrangement.

Char	"H"	"E"	"L"	"L"	"O"	[Space]	"Y"	"O"	"U"	"O"	"K"	"A"	"Y"	NONE
Value (Dec)	72	69	75	75	79	32	89	79	213 (=85+128)	79	75	65	217 (=89+128)	255
Offset	0	1	2	3	4	5	6	7	8	9	10	11	12	13

We have only two messages "Hello You" and "Okay" in this catalog. Each of the messages is terminated by a byte with bit 7 set: bit 7 is always 0 in ASCII codes, so to indicate that a character is the last one in the string, we retain the code, but we add 128 (binary weight of bit 7) to it to show it's the last character (as in the case of "U" and "Y" in Table 3-2). When we read the value 255 as the first byte of a message, it means we have reached the end of the catalog.

The help message is implemented as a catalog with just one single message incorporating newlines where needed, but the messages catalog and the word list/dictionary are multientry catalogs. To retrieve a message from a catalog you simply need to know the entry number (e.g., in Table 3-2, the string "Hello You" would be entry #0 and the string "Okay" would be entry #2). We'll see how this works in more detail in the section "WordDune Sketch Code Walk".

Although CatBuilder reserves EEPROM space for the word list/dictionary catalog, it's actually the WordDune sketch that initializes it to the default set of words, if it hasn't already been done.

WordDune Sketch Code Walk

The following code walk summarizes each of the functions within the WordDune program. Please refer to the program sources themselves, available from www.apress.com/9781430244462.

WordDune: Declarations Section

This section sets up various operation parameters and constants. Of interest might be

- DO_FORMAT which causes the EEPROM contents to be reinitialized.

- WORDS_PER_LEVEL which allows you to set more or fewer words to be spotted at each level.

- The initial set of words comes from the declaration of the array firstWords. If you don't want to use the TTL serial channel to expand your word list you can expand this array with additional or different words and then set up the game again (as per earlier instructions).

- levelData, which is an array of values that set the timing parameters for each level of the game. See the comments embedded in the program code for what these mean.

setup()

In the setup function the serial channel is initialized, the LCD screen parameters set up, and the screen cleared. The switch port is made into an input, and the pull-up on it is enabled (by writing HIGH to it). Then, if there are no words yet in the dictionary, or DO_FORMAT is true, we format the word list area of the EEPROM. We then check if there are a usable number of words and output a message saying how many words there are using sayMessage(). The current game level is set to 0; the serial channel gets a "WordDune" prompt sent to it.

Because the game makes use of random selections at several points, we need a random element to seed the random number generator. What we do is read a value from the floating analog input 2 which will be some random value based on whatever electrical mush that input is picking up at that moment. We use that as the random seed to ensure we get different random numbers each time we play. Then, we transfer control to doSplashScreen() which does pretty stuff on the LCD screen, all the while inviting the user to click the press button to play a game. When a user does this, then, the splash screen returns control to setup(), we clear the LCD screen, and setup() ends, transferring control to the main loop().

loop()

In the main loop of the program, we select four random words (issuing an error message and going into a terminal loop if there are not enough words available to do so). Then, having selected the words, we call the level introducer, which does all the onscreen stuff to gently take a user into a game level. After waiting for the click switch to be released, we enter the main part of the level loop.

In the main part of the loop we loop around very fast, putting individual characters on the screen at random locations. To choose the individual characters, we use a switch case block, casing off the current game level, to choose a random character according to the game level: at first it's spaces and symbols, which makes it far easier to spot complete uppercase words among them, but for the higher levels it's a mix of lower- and uppercase letters and then eventually it's all uppercase letters, among which it's very hard to spot complete words. Every now and again, by seeing if a randomly generated number matches a preset value, we put one of our chosen complete words on the screen. Just before the end of each loop we check to see if the user has pressed the button. It's part of the game spec that they don't have to wait until the end of a level to see the list of words they were supposed to have spotted—they can end the level early if they think they already know the words. Also, at the end of each loop we check to see if there has been any input from the serial channel and we go process anything that has arrived.

When all four words have been shown for the configured number of times, the level ends. We do the levelEnd() function (which prompts the user to say what words he has spotted, and then shows him what words were actually duned during this level). We then clear the LCD screen and bump the level counter. If the level just ended was the last, highest level, the user is told game over and invited to play again and the game restarts at level 0. Otherwise we loop around again to play the next level in sequence.

format_EEPROM()

Args: Size and StartByte

This function fills the indicated section of the EEPROM with all ones (0xFF). The fill operation starts from StartByte and goes on until EEPROM address Size is reached.

addToDictionary()

Args: theWord

This function appends the provided ASCII-coded word to the end of the word list (dictionary). It fails if the word already exists, if it was invalid, or if the WordList catalog is full.

dumpEEPROMToSerialChannel()

Args: None

This function outputs a hex dump (Hex and ASCII format) of the EEPROM contents to the serial channel (see Figure 3-17).

```
0000:  06 00 ee 00 7d 01 0a 0d 0a 57 6f 72 64 20 44 75    ....}....Word Du
0010:  6e 65 3a 20 56 65 72 73 69 6f 6e a0 42 61 73 65    ne: Version.Base
0020:  20 64 69 63 74 69 6f 6e 61 72 79 20 72 65 62 75     dictionary rebu
0030:  69 6c f4 3d 3d 3d 3d 3d 3d bd 20 65 6e 74 72 69    il.======. entri
0040:  65 73 20 66 6f 75 6e 64 ae 20 46 72 65 65 20 73    es found. Free s
0050:  70 61 63 65 20 3d a0 57 6f 72 64 20 77 61 73 20    pace =.Word was
0060:  61 64 64 65 e4 57 6f 72 64 20 4e 4f 54 20 61 64    adde.Word NOT ad
0070:  64 65 64 3a a0 49 6e 73 75 66 66 69 63 69 65 6e    ded:.Insufficien
0080:  74 20 73 70 61 63 65 ae 44 69 63 74 69 6f 6e 61    t space.Dictiona
0090:  72 79 20 63 6f 72 72 75 70 74 bf 4d 69 6e 69 6d    ry corrupt.Minim
00a0:  75 6d 20 63 68 61 72 20 63 6f 75 6e 74 20 69 73    um char count is
00b0:  a0 4e 6f 74 20 61 64 64 65 64 3a 20 45 72 72 6f    .Not added: Erro
00c0:  72 20 63 6f 64 65 20 3d a0 55 6e 6b 6e 6f 77 6e    r code =.Unknown
00d0:  20 63 6d 64 ae 4e 6f 20 73 75 63 68 20 77 6f 72     cmd.No such wor
00e0:  64 a1 57 6f 72 64 20 65 78 69 73 74 73 a1 43 6f    d.Word exists.Co
00f0:  6d 6d 61 6e 64 73 3a 0a 0d 41 44 44 20 5b 57 6f    mmands:..ADD [Wo
0100:  72 64 5d 3a 20 41 64 64 20 6e 65 77 20 77 6f 72    rd]: Add new wor
0110:  64 0a 0d 44 45 50 3a 20 44 75 6d 70 20 45 45 50    d..DEP: Dump EEP
0120:  52 4f 4d 0a 0d 44 49 43 3a 20 4c 69 73 74 20 64    ROM..DIC: List d
0130:  69 63 74 69 6f 6e 61 72 79 0a 0d 4c 45 56 3a 20    ictionary..LEV:
0140:  73 65 74 2f 73 68 6f 77 20 67 61 6d 65 20 6c 65    set/show game le
0150:  76 65 6c 0a 0d 44 45 4c 3a 20 44 65 6c 65 74 65    vel..DEL: Delete
0160:  20 77 6f 72 64 0a 0d 53 57 43 3a 20 53 68 6f 77     word..SWC: Show
0170:  20 77 6f 72 64 20 63 6f 75 6e 74 0a 8d 53 55 50     word count..SUP
```

Figure 3-17. *WordDune: Output from the dump EEPROM (DEP) command*

The DEP command is mainly useful for debug purposes.

dumpDictToSerialChannel()

Args: None

This function outputs a formatted list of words in the dictionary/word list to the serial channel. Figure 3-18 illustrates the output.

```
Word Dune: Version 3.0b
Base dictionary rebuilt
WordDune> DIC
======
01) SUPERIOR
02) CLIFF
03) INFLUENZA
04) PACIFIC
05) MADRIGAL
06) POWERHOUSE
07) CANADA
08) MATRIX
09) GENEROUS
10) ALBATROSS
 Free space = 567
WordDune>
```

Figure 3-18. *WordDune: Output from the Dictionary command*

The table below describes the less major functions of the program.

NAME	ARGS	Description
returnDictWordCount()	None	This function returns an integer indicating the number of words currently in the word list/dictionary. It can return zero, if the list is empty.
getDictWord()	wordNum, byteArray	This function returns the wordNumth word from the list by writing it into the byte array. If there is no word at index wordNum then it returns -1 to indicate an error
doInputBufferParser()	None	This function is called when a terminating character (return key) has been received via the serial line. This function looks at the contents of the input buffer and tries to resolve it into an actionable command. If it finds a command, it actions it with the appropriate program functions. If no match is found, it just puts out an "unrecognized command" response.
processKeyboardChar()	theChar	Each time the serial line receives a character this function is called. If the received character is a normal printable character it is converted to uppercase (if it's a letter), it is echoed back to the serial channel and it is placed into the next available slot in the input buffer. If it's not a normal printable character then the function checks to see if it's a terminator (return), in which case doInputBufferParser is called. If it's a backspace then the rubout routine is run. If it's CTRL/R the contents of the input buffer are echoed back out to the serial channel.

(continued)

NAME	ARGS	Description
`sayMessage()`	`catNumber,` `msgNumber, outMsg,` `doNewLine`	This function first retrieves the indicated message number from the indicated catalog. (0 = messages, 1 = help, dictionary = 2). If `outMsg` == true then the retrieved message is sent out to the serial channel, ending with a newline if indicated by the `doNewLine` arg. If `outMsg` is false then the message is only retrieved but nothing is done with it. This is purely to provide a debug tool for checking if a message exists. Returns an empty message if the requested message was found, or a generic error message if it was not.
`returnZeroPacked NumberString()`	`number,` `desiredNumber Length`	This function returns a string representation of the indicated number front-padded with zeroes to make it up to the indicated length. So, for example, `returnZeroPackedNumberString` (3,3) would return "003." Returns an empty string if there was a problem. Note: We could have used `sprintf()` for this, but that would have used more memory.
`returnFreeEEPROM Space()`	`EEPROM_LEN`	This function returns an integer indicating how many free bytes remain in the EEPROM. The arg tells it the overall size of the EEPROM (since this cannot easily be discovered dynamically). In effect, due to the way the catalogs in EEPROM are structured, the number returned from this function indicates how many more characters can be added to the dictionary/word list

(continued)

NAME	ARGS	Description
doDeleteWord()	wordToZap	This function deletes the indicated word from the dictionary/word list and fills in the empty space it leaves behind to maintain the integrity of the catalog. The argument wordToZap can be sent as "*" (asterisk) meaning delete *all* words. The user is appropriately prompted to confirm any delete action. The function returns true or false according to whether the word delete(s) went ahead or not.
returnWordLocation()	theWord	This function is a utility for other functions. It returns the EEPROM offset location of a word in the catalog. Returns -1 if the word was not found.
returnDictionaryBase()	None	This function is a utility for other functions. It returns the EEPROM address where the dictionary/word list begins.
doLevelIntroducer()	levelNumber, wordCount	This function does all the messaging and prompting necessary to introduce the user of the game to a new level. The level number being introduced and the number of words available for use are indicated in the args. The function only returns when it detects that a user has pressed the push button.
selectFourWords()	None	This function selects four unique words from the dictionary/word list. These are placed in the duneWords array. If there are insufficient words available it returns -1
findNumberInWordArray()	numToFind	Utility function used by others. Returns true if the word array already contains the indicated word number.

(continued)

NAME	ARGS	Description
chooseRandomWord IndexIndex()	None	Utility function used by others. Returns the index of a duneWord that has not yet been shown four times during the current level.
returnTotalTryCount()	None	Utility function used by others. Returns an integer indicating how many complete words have been shown during the current level.
doLevelEnd()	None	Utility function used by others. Does everything required at the end of a game level. Tells the user the level has ended, prompts her to click when she is ready to see the word list and then awaits a further click to proceed to next level or game end.
showDuneWords()	onSerial, onLCD, pastTense	A function that shows the duneWords for the current level. The list of words is put out on the serial port and on to the LCD screen as indicated by the args. Uses current (words are. . .") or past tense ("words were . . .") according to the arg. The latter is mainly meant for debug use
sayThis()	whatToSay, onSerial, onLCD, serialGetsNewLine	A function that puts out a message on the serial port and and/or to the LCD screen as indicated by the args. The serialGetsNewLine arg allows partial messages to be put out and subsequently appended to by others.
awaitKeypress()	timeoutMs, returnWhenPressed, digitalPinNum	A function that will await a use key press for the indicated number of milliseconds (0 means wait forever). Returns either when the timeout period expires or when the button is pressed (returnWhenPressed == true) or when the button has been pressed and then released (returnWhenPressed == false)

(continued)

NAME	ARGS	Description
doSplashScreen()	None	Does a selection of eye-catching and pretty things on the LCD screen while waiting for the user to press the button to start a game. In arcade game terms this is an attractor sequence.
fillScreenWith RandomCharacters()	None	A utility function used by doSplashScreen(). Does what the name suggests!
doSerialInput()	None	Checks for an incoming character on the serial channel, if any is found calls processKeyboardCharacter to buffer the received character. It calls the input buffer parses if the character is a terminator.

That concludes our code walk, and our description of the game WordDune. Have fun with it!

Summary

In this chapter we have looked at a game of observation called WordDune. We looked at the hardware, the game play, and the software. We looked at how you can customize the game by adding your own words to it. We also took a detailed code walk.

Coming Up Next

Project 4: The Lighting Waterfall.

CHAPTER 4

■ ■ ■

Project 4: The Lighting Waterfall

Light the Way—Ever So Prettily!

In this chapter we look at a project that is not only useful but pretty. If you have a passageway or corridor or even a long, thin room in your home that could do with some nice lighting, then this could be the project for you.

People used to expect very little of the lighting in their homes. One nice bright light in the middle of the room, a simple on/off switch, and the job was done. The fact that our parents and grandparents were happy with this kind of lighting was probably a reflection of the fact that *their* forefathers had to spend their darkness hours trying to read or work by feeble gaslights or even candlelight: so, to them, being able to make a room as bright as daylight whenever they wanted must have seemed like a dream come true. Viva Edison and Swann!

But pretty soon people realized that controlled and varied lighting could greatly enhance and transform even a very plain room: the more chic lighting styles of the 1950s and 1960s were born. Semiconductor technology entered the scene when–in the 1970s–it became possible to make a light dimmer that would fit into the footprint of a standard wall switch. Now, you could not only place lights strategically to enhance a room, you could set their brightness to whatever you wanted. Why not have several lights? Have some with plain white lamps in, and perhaps some different colored ones to create different pools of light within the room.

A steady stream of incremental developments to lighting followed that continues to this day. If you could make a device that would allow people to manually control the brightness of their lights, why couldn't you give them an IR remote control, so that they could do it from their seat? If you could remotely control the state and brightness of all the lights in a room, why couldn't you give control of those functions to an automated system? If that system could be given access to "people sensors," why couldn't the lights automatically come on when someone entered the room and go off a little while after the last person left it? Do you need different lighting setups in the room for different times of the day, or days of the week? No problem; the control system could be made to remember "scenes": each scene can have preset color combinations, brightness settings, even light directions if you add a motorized direction setting to the light fittings.

In more recent times, the LED–previously thought of mostly as an indicator light or for making seven-segment displays for clocks or technical equipment–suddenly got brighter and jazzier. Developments such as Professor Shuji Nakamura's invention of the blue LED in the mid-1990s (he also perfected bright LEDs in green and white colors) made LEDs a serious contender for the filament lamp's crown as light source of choice. LED lights use a great deal less electricity than conventional lighting methods, and they have a much longer lifetime. However, LED lighting was initially far more expensive than traditional lighting. This is partly because LEDs work on low-voltage DC, not high-voltage mains AC and so the additional cost of providing a converter is involved, but the price difference is also due to higher production costs. Also, LED light gives a different, more directional light than the lights we have been used to, which has met with some consumer resistance. However, with innovations such as "warm" LED lighting, better diffusers, and ever higher intensity devices, plus the ever increasing cost of domestic electricity and desire for more lighting control, the advance of LED lighting has been slow but relentless–to the point where it's no longer impossible to imagine a time when most homes will be mainly lit by LED lighting.

One characteristic of LED lighting is that it often aggregates lots of small LEDs to form a light source. For example, the LED work light pictured (assembled and disassembled) in Figure 4-1 uses 72 pure white LEDs to provide a bright directional work light[1] from a 6V battery source. In the case of this particular light all the LEDs come on at the same time and brightness; this is just a work light. However, in other products, LED lights intended for use as disco light shows or ambient lighting components for restaurants, LEDs are organized into groups or banks of lights to give very fine control over lighting levels and sequencing.

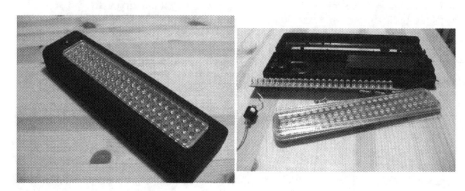

Figure 4-1. *72 LED worklight*

When you bring this together with the ability of an MCU to exercise detailed control over a large number of individual LEDs or sets of LEDs, you can suddenly see the possibility of exercising endlessly detailed variable control over room lighting schemes and doing things that, previously, were prohibitively complex or expensive.

The project we're about to see is but one example . . .

---

[1]Such products are a very cheap source of LEDs by the way, if you are careful with your desoldering.

The Passageway Light

Most homes have some kind of hallway, corridor, or passageway, either inside or as a covered way outside. Some homes have long, thin rooms which can be difficult to light with any style. When we moved into our house, the 16-foot (5 meters) passageway that goes along the middle of it was lit by a single pendant, an unshaded bulb hanging from the ceiling. The switch for this light was at one end of the passageway. It let you see where you were going, but it received zero points for eye appeal, convenience, and style. I wondered what I could do to light this space better: this project (or, more precisely, projects, since we'll also see the design for a MKII version) was the result.

I'm a great believer in the interior designer's notion that if you want to give a room some style, you must light it with indirect light sources. Okay, you do still need to have a brash, bright light available for cleaning, decorating, looking for a lost key, and so on, but take a cue from the hospitality industry! Most clubs, restaurants, and bars have fluorescent tubes on the ceiling, but they're only there so that the cleaners and maintenance staff can see what they're doing—and those places can look pretty plain and ugly in that mode. There's a reason we refer to the "cold light of day"! However, when serving their main purpose, being a party place, the plain lights go off and the atmosphere lighting takes over—usually making the place look superb. Why should the relaxation rooms of your home be any different? Cold but bright lights for working in them (found that key yet?) and softer, more varied, lights for when you're relaxing in them. So, I started with the idea that these would be hidden, indirect lights.

Nobody stays in the passageway, people only pass through on their way to one of the other rooms, and so my next design goal was that the lights should come on when needed but automatically go off again after some fixed amount of time. Then, inspired by the long, thin nature of the space, I seized on the idea of a lighting waterfall; the lights would come on in sequence along the line of the passageway and go off in sequence again when the time-out was reached. Since there were entrances at both ends of the passageway, why couldn't the waterfall come on in the direction of travel? Could the lights fade in and fade out, rather than clicking on or off one by one? Whoa! Suddenly I had a spec in my head for this project!

I was convinced early on that this was going to be a LED lighting scheme. At this time, RGB (Red Green Blue) LED strips were still pretty expensive, but I was quite taken with some flexible LED lights strips that I bought from an online auction site. Being, I think, intended for used on vehicles, these run on 12V DC and seem to be completely waterproof. They can be flexed into pretty much any shape you might need.

I decided to use these for the project and so I bought some single color strips, like the one shown in Figure 4-2, from a well-known Internet auction site. These are available in different lengths containing 12, 24, 30, or 48 LEDs on a flexible PCB set inside a very flexible plastic gel casing. Alternative sources of supply are

- www.bestlightingbuy.com/motorcycle-led-strip-car-lights-flexible-grill-light.html (United States).

- www.brightlightz.co.uk/categories/led-strip-lights-flexible (UK).

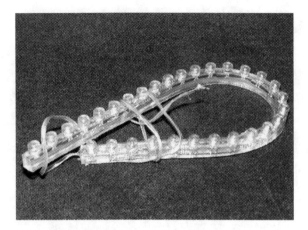

Figure 4-2. Flexible single color LED strip

There is, of course, no reason why you should not use SMD (Surface Mount Device) LED strips–cut to your desired length–in your implementation, in which case you would probably need:

- www.sparkfun.com (search for COM-10259; they do many others too) (United States).

- www.maplin.co.uk (search for stock number N56CF, and others) (UK).

This was so obviously a job for an MCU that I never considered any other implementation approach, but that requirement for the LEDs to fade in and out gave me a problem. The ATmega328 that I wanted to use for this project offers four pins with usable hardware PWM capability. These are

- Pin 5 (Arduino D3).

- Pin 15 (Arduino D9).

- Pin 16 (Arduino D10).

- Pin 17 (Arduino D11).

Pins 11 and 12 (Arduino pins D5 and D6, respectively) also offer PWM; however, as noted on the Arduino web site, the millis() and delay() functions of the Arduino software share the same internal timer used to generate PWM on those pins and so when used at low-duty cycles these pins may not fully turn off. Well, we need a reliable black level for this project and we make extensive use of the delay() function in its software; therefore, it seems sensible to stick to using just the PWM pins that can be guaranteed to behave as expected.

All of the above meant that I could only drive four LED strips from the MCU in the way that the spec called for. After a lot of thought, I decided that I would go ahead and build a four-way setup and see how it looked and revisit the project for a MKII approach if necessary.

The project requirements were

- To provide a set of four LED lighting strips (I eventually settled on warm yellow as the LED color, mainly because the walls of the passageway are painted white and would mix well with it).

- To have each lighting strip's brightness be independently software controllable and dimmable between nothing and full brightness using PWM.

- To provide a "person detector" at either end of the passageway which, when triggered, will turn on the lights for a preset 40 seconds.

- To have the lights to come on and go off in a waterfall sequence, starting at the end at which a person enters the passageway. At the end of the time-out sequence, lights go off in the same sequence they came on (i.e., first off is the one that was first on).

- To put the lights permanently on at full intensity via a manual button on the control box.

- To turn the lights off permanently, via a button on the control box, so that they cannot be triggered.

I elected to use two Paradox PA-461 PIR sensors as the "people sensor" elements in this project. These can be obtained at quite low cost if you shop around. You can find a lot of details about these sensors in Chapter 4 of *Practical AVR Microcontrollers* (Apress, 2012), so I won't recap here. Suffice it to say that you feed the sensors a +12-volt supply and they momentarily break a closed loop contact whenever anyone walks past them. If you can't get these particular sensors, it doesn't matter; your local vendor or favorite online source should be able to supply something similar.

For the purposes of this project I refer to the sensors as

- Sensor 1–also called the "near sensor" because it is near the control box

- Sensor 2—also called the "far sensor" because it is not near the control box

The physical layout diagram in Figure 4-7 makes this arrangement clear.

Proving Circuit

In order to develop the software for this project and to refine the hardware design I used the circuit diagram shown in Figure 4-2 to build up the design on the test bed –as built in Chapter 2 of *Practical AVR Microcontrollers* (Apress, 2012). If you want to try this design out for yourself, follow this circuit diagram.

As you can see, there is nothing special about it; it uses a ULN2803A Darlington transistor array chip to allow the AVR to drive the LED strips. Each of my LED strips (24 LEDs per strip) uses about 220 ma at 12V, which is well within the capabilities of the 2803, but your LED strip consumption may vary, so check with the vendor before you buy. Some longer (48 LED) strips pull quite a lot more current, so you need to make sure you don't go above about 350 ma per driver or you may get into heat problems with the 2803 and start needing to fit a heatsink.

The circuit diagram shows the MCU as an ATmega328, but originally this used an ATmega168: they are pin-compatible devices, the 168 just has less memory, but that should not matter in this application: if you have an ATmega168 and want to use it, give it a try!

Whichever MCU you use, you should make sure it's running at 8 MHz. Running the MCU at the "out of the box" speed of 1 MHz is not sufficient in this application; it is too slow. If you're not sure how to set your AVR to run at 8 MHz, see the discussion on AVRDude and the CKDIV8 fuse in "AVRDude Out of the Box" in Chapter 3 of *Practical AVR Microcontrollers* (Apress, 2012).

As the circuit diagram in Figure 4-3 shows, the four outputs of the AVR which are capable of hardware PWM are used to drive the inputs of the ULN2803A driver chip and therefore the LED strips. The remaining, unused, driver stages on the 2803 have their bases (5B-8B) grounded.

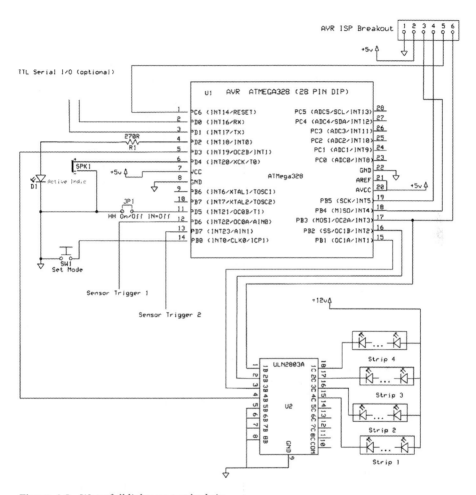

Figure 4-3. *Waterfall lights on test bed rig*

Mostly this will be used as an automatic system, and so the control box is tucked away somewhere unobtrusive. Therefore, rather than use multiple buttons, I decided to have just one push button and to use it to step through the three (plus one) possible controller modes.

- *Automatic mode*: Sensors trigger lights to fade up in appropriate order according to which sensor triggers them.

- *ON mode*: Lights come on and stay on.

- *OFF mode*: Lights go off and stay off–even if sensor triggers received.

- *A "pretties" mode*: The LED sets fade up and down in quick alternation. This is the "Easter egg" feature of this program–you get into it by holding down the mode button for about seven seconds until the unit bleeps. Nothing spectacular, but something to surprise your friends or family with, especially once they have gotten used to the normal functions.

The downside of using only one button is that the unit needs to signal to the user which mode is being selected at each button press. For this purpose I added a small piezo speaker. It can be directly attached to an AVR pin and can, if installed properly, be easily loud enough for making the required bleeping noises inside a box. The speaker emits

- A rising tone when a button press sets the unit into Automatic mode.

- A constant pitch tone when entering ON mode.

- A falling tone when entering OFF mode.

I did toy with the idea of having the unit do a short beep whenever the sensors sent in a trigger pulse, but I quickly concluded (based on experience in the past) that such a feature would quickly get to be annoying.

I added a heartbeat LED connected to pin 4 of the MCU (Arduino pin D2). This is just a single LED that is pulsed on and off once per second by the program (and just blips very briefly when the unit is in OFF mode). This is handy as a visual confirmation that the software is still running and on the rails!

I also added a jumper, JP1: This is intended to let the software know whether or not it is being used with an integrated home help "smart home" system. When this jumper is IN (i.e., the two contacts are bridged) then the software will not expect to output status information on its serial channel to a superior system. This is largely a future-oriented feature, not of immediate use.

Whether or not the unit thinks it is participating in a larger "smart home" setup, it will always accept incoming commands from the serial channel. Most of these were originally for helping with test purposes (e.g., to be able to simulate sensor activations when no sensors were actually wired up to the initial version built up on the test rig). However, many of them are useful to keep in the mix for troubleshooting the unit, should any problems occur. I originally envisaged just one or two commands, but by the time I had completed the software, the command set had grown. The following table lists the commands in the finished software,

Command	Effect
ALLOFF	All LED strips go off and stay off.
ALLON	All LED strips come on and stay on at full brightness.
BEEP	Makes the unit beep. Useful to ensure the unit is still operating properly.
CLOCK	Shows the system time, this is how many milliseconds since the unit started.

(continued)

Command	Effect
CYCLE	The unit enters FADECYCLE mode for 1.5 times the length of the period set for sensor triggering.
FDN	Fade Down: all LEDs fade from maximum brightness to off.
FUP	Fade UP: all LEDs fade up from minimum to maximum brightness.
Ixxx	Intensity. Sets all LED strips to the indicated intensity level, where xxx is a number from 0 to 255. Illegal values are ignored.
SPP	Show PWM Parameters. Prints a table of the current PWM settings for each LED strip
Txx	Trigger: Simulates a trigger from an external sensor. xx should 01 or 02 according to the sensor to be simulated.

Waterfall Lights Software

The final software for the MKI waterfall lights (then still called the "passageway lights") was version 2.0a. The software is rather too big to reproduce in full here, but it is downloadable from the book's web site (www.apress.com/9781430244462). The following is a function-by-function code walk summary of the software:

Function Name	Args/return type	Commentary
Global header	None/void	In the global header section of this program a set of hardware related constants are declared. For example, these set pin numbers for items like the BUTTON and the SOUNDER.
		Then the constants for the three different available fade rates are set.
		The SEQUENCE_STAGGER constant is declared to be 500 milliseconds: this determines the speed of the waterfall effect (i.e., the time delay between each LED strip down the line being taken to its next level of brightness during a fade up or fade down).
		Then the sensor count is declared. You could just run this with one sensor if you wanted to.

(*continued*)

Function Name	Args/return type	Commentary
		Constants are declared for the various light modes that the LED strips can enter. Only FADEIN, FADEOUT, FADECYCLE, and ON and OFF are actually implemented in this version.
		After explaining PWM, the main data structure used by the program—a LIGHT_STRUCT—is defined and an instance of it (the lights[ ] array) is created and filled with details such as pin numbers that control each light represented in the array. All PWM values are set to zero, meaning all lights start as off.
		Next, constants are declared to define things like how many lights are being controlled and how long they stay on when triggered.
		After defining the program modes and the push-button long press duration (for the Easter egg) and doing a few more initializations and declarations, the header is done.
setup()	None/void	In the setup() function the various pins required for the control button, the LED strip drivers, the heartbeat LED, the sense pin, etc., are all set to the appropriate pin type, INPUT or OUTPUT. All input pins have their pull-up resistors enabled by writing a HIGH to them.
		The smart home help jumper is read to see if that mode is needed.
		The serial channel is initialized and an announcement sent to it with the program version number and build date.
		Finally, the power up sound is made on the internal speaker.

(continued)

Function Name	Args/return type	Commentary
loop()	None	The program now enters the main loop. For various reasons, we don't want the loop() function to continually reinitialize at each loop in the usual way. So all the code in the loop() function is run inside a do-while loop that can never end. It will run round until forever, but without reinitializing any of loop()'s resources as it otherwise would. We could use static variables but. . . nah!
		The loop starts by calling the doSerialInput() function (see below in this table)
		Then, it looks to see if the mode button is pressed. If the button is NOT pressed now, but it was pressed last time we checked, then we check if it was a long press (Easter egg) or a normal press. If it was a normal length press, we call the shortPress() function, or the longPress() function if not.
		If the button IS pressed now, we check to see how long it's been pressed for and action a longPress() if that is called for.
		If the button is pressed now, but was not pressed last time we looked, then we remember the time now: this, when the button is released in future, allows us to know how long it was pressed for.
		Next the program checks the sensor inputs. If the program is in normal (automatic) mode and a sensor is found to have been triggered then the sensorEvent() function is called. The sensors used in the prototype stay active for about one second, easily long enough for the main loop to spot their activation. Different sensors with shorter activation durations might need some adjustment to this approach.

(*continued*)

Function Name	Args/return type	Commentary
		Now, the program enters the lights processing loop. Inside this, the required state of the lights–as represented by the contents of the lights[] array–are made real by writing out each light's PWM state to the pin that controls it. Individual lights can be set to enter different modes in future, principally in the fadeCycle() function (see below in this table). We next check to see if any such change is pending for the current light and action it if so.
		Turn-off times for lights are processed, and the lights processing loop ends.
		If the 100th-of-a-second function is due to be run it is invoked now. The hundredthSec() function does fade advances and other things – see below in this table.
oneSec()	None/void	The oneSec() function is called once per second from hundredthSec(); it pulses the heartbeat (a.k.a. "active") LED at a rate appropriate to the current mode of operation (once per second for normal, very short bursts of light for OFF.
hundredthSec()	None/void	hundredthSec() is a function that is called once every 100th of a second from loop(). It acts as a dispatcher for once per second events and for lights processing events (such as fade progressions and control changes). The various lighting modes (FADEIN, etc.) are implemented in a switch table within this function. Important to realize that this function only works on the lights[] array, it does not directly change the pin states–that only happens in the main loop() as we saw above.

(continued)

Function Name	Args/return type	Commentary
doInputBuffer Parser()	None/Boolean	doInputBufferParser() is called from doSerialInput() when that function recognizes it has received a terminator character. This function uses a switch table to try to recognize one of the implemented command and checks the supplied command line arguments (if any are needed) before it calls the required command's implementation function. Unknown commands get the "unknown command" response, and commands that fail to return a success value, or command line arguments that are incorrect in some way all result in a "Cannot execute command" message. The function returns TRUE if the command succeeded or FALSE if not.
showPwmParameters()	None/void	This function simply prints a short report out to the serial channel showing contents of the lights[] array.
sensorEvent()	Int sensorNum / Boolean	The sensorEvent() function carries out the light sequencing when a sensor trigger is received. Triggers only have effect if the lights are currently OFF. If the lights are already active, nothing is changed and the function returns FALSE.
		The currentState of lights[0] is sampled to determine whether the lights are OFF at the time of the trigger.
		The lights are programmed to fade up in a time-staggered sequence starting from now.
		If the sensorNum is 1 then the lights fade in the array order 0,1,2,3
		If the sensor number is 2, then they switch on in descending order.
		When a trigger has been accepted and actioned the function returns TRUE.
doBeep()	None/void	The sounder makes a steady one KHz tone for half a second.

(continued)

Function Name	Args/return type	Commentary
setFadeCycleMode()	None/Boolean	If the current mode is not INACTIVE (i.e., OFF) then this function puts the lights into FadeCycle mode for one minute.
		If the unit is currently in INACTIVE mode, then the function returns FALSE.
		The function acts upon the lights[] array, not the hardware directly and returns TRUE when the mode has been set.
		This function is called from the longPress() function.
longPress()	Unsigned long pressDuration /void	This function is called from loop() when a long button press is deemed to have occurred. In fact in this version it simply calls setFadeCycleMode() and doesn't use its arg.
shortPress()	None/void	This function advances the current program mode by one, wrapping back to the first mode if needs be. It invokes other functions to make appropriate bleeps and noises for the new mode.
doPowerUpSound()	None/void	This function sounds a rising note sound to indicate a power up or activation.
doPowerDownSound()	None/void	This function sounds a falling note sound to indicate a deactivation.
doSerialInput()	None/void	In this function we check for any incoming characters on the serial channel. It uses processKeyboardChar() to assess the incoming character (see below in this table).
		If the incoming character is a terminator, then the input buffer is tailed with a zero byte to make it into a complete zero terminated string and the parser (see above in this table) is called. Upon return from the parser, the input buffer is reinitialized, and a fresh user prompt is issued, to invite more commands.

(continued)

Function Name	Args/return type	Commentary
process KeyboardChar()	Char the Char/int	This function actions an ASCII input character received as its arg. It buffers the char, if it's a printable one. If it's a control char, then it actions it if possible, or ignores it. It also processes backspaces (which it treats as a rubout character) and CTRL/R to show and reprint the input buffer contents. If it's a CR char, then the function returns 1, else it returns zero.
turnAllOn()	None/void	Processes the lights[] array to turn all the LEDs full on. This will be implemented shortly afterward in the main loop.
turnAllOff()	None/void	Processes the lights[] array to turn all the LEDs off. This will be implemented shortly afterward in the main loop.
showSystemTime()	None/void	Sends out a formatted message to the serial channel to show the system time—in this context, this means the number of milliseconds since the AVR was started, not the wall clock time.

So, having worked out the hardware and software the next step is the implementation and installation.

Moving to Making It

Moving into the maker stage of the project, the first thing I had to decide was how to house the lights. If you want to build this project you'll have to decide this too; your decision, like mine, will be based on the characteristics of the installation site.

In my case, the walls of the passageway are very uneven, being rendered in a style known as "roughcast," which does not provide a uniform, smooth surface. My original idea was to build a small wall-mounted pelmeted box out of long lengths of stripwood. This would hide the lights themselves but allow the light to shine downward from under the pelmet. However, I decided that an assembly of stripwoods might not be flexible enough to follow the ins and outs of my wall.

After some thought, I came up with the idea of using a square plastic wire channel with a snap-on lid (a.k.a. plastic cable trunking). This wire channel was not only flexible enough to follow the contours of my wall pretty closely, but it also came in white plastic, so it would blend in with the white painted wall better than wood. Although it is harder to find, I believe you can also get it in other colors such as brown and black. This kind of channel (which is often self-adhesive via sticky tape on the back) comes both in fixed lengths (usually 10- or 11-feet lengths) and in flat form, in a roll that you can make it up from. You can easily cut it to the required length with a hacksaw.

Figure 4-4 shows a section of this stuff, which is sold in most electrical contractor outlets, DIY stores, and even in more general online stores like Amazon.

Figure 4-4. *White plastic cable channel with snap-on lid in place*

I used a hacksaw blade and a safety craft knife to cut out slots in one side of this wire channel to form the light outlets–sized to the LED strips.

To suspend the LED strips from the top of the channel, I drilled pairs of very small holes–just enough to get a strand of plastic-coated (must be coated) garden wire through. I looped the garden wire around the LED strip and on the outside of the channel I twisted and knotted the two ends of the garden wire to securely hold the LED strip in place. These twists should be tight, but obviously not so tight as to chew into the LED strip. The strips protrude from the top, but since the assembly will be mounted high up, they cannot normally be seen. The diagram in Figure 4-5 shows the general idea (see also the photo later in Figure 4-16). You could simply glue the LED strips into place inside the assembly if you wanted to, but that would make any future maintenance, changes, or update activities harder than they need to be.

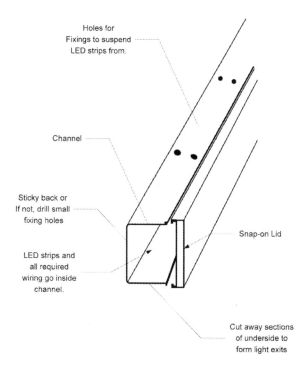

Figure 4-5. Waterfall light holder assembly

Figure 4-5 visualizes these points.

Having installed the LED strips into the channel I then got a 5 amp wire and ran it the length of the holder. This forms the +12-volt feed for the four LED strips and the far-end sensor. I cut each LED strip's positive wire into this +12V feed wire. Of course, each cut-in point has to be taped up or shrink-wrapped to prevent any mishaps. In addition to the +12V feed wire, I then ran a six-way ribbon cable along the whole length of the holder and out the other side. The six conductors in this ribbon cable are used as follows:

- Wire 1 drops off at LED strip #1 and connects to its negative wire.

- Wire 2 drops off at LED strip #2 and connects to its negative wire.

- Wire 3 drops off at LED strip #3 and connects to its negative wire.

- Wire 4 drops off at LED strip #4 and connects to its negative wire.

- Wire 5 extends out to the far sensor and provides its "trigger" line back into the control box.

- Wire 6 carries a ground connection to the far sensor power feed, and to one side of its normally closed relay contacts. The +12V wire is also extended out to the far sensor to provide its power feed.

With the light holder assembly made, the next order of business is connections. The control box needed the following connection groups:

- A connector to bring in the signals from the light holder assembly–this had to be at least a seven-way connector. (+12V feed, four LED strip return wires, ground, and the far sensor trigger line).

- A connector for the near sensor–a three-way connector.

- A power connector to bring in 12V DC at about 2 amps. I decided that in the implementation, rather than having dual supplies or batteries it would be sensible to just feed the control box with +12V from a mains adaptor and have it incorporate a regulator that makes the MCU's required +5 volts from that.

If you're building your own version of this project you can decide to use whatever connectors you want, provided they can provide the right number of connections (as listed above) and each pole of the connector can carry at least one amp.

In my case, after initially considering a seven-way DIN connector from

- www.mouser.com (stock number 568-NYS323) (international)

- www.maplin.co.uk (stock number HH30H) (UK)

I decided to look for something with more connections, in case I decided to add more lights. I eventually settled on using a military style 14-way connector. I found out that these are very good quality and you can get the plug and socket for around $10 (delivered price) from several online sites. If you search for Y2M14-TK or Y2M14-ZJ you will find them for sale by many sellers[2]: you'll also sometimes find them listed as "Aviation connectors," "Y2M connectors," or "CA-Bayonet connectors."

If you do use one of these connectors, be aware that the plug hood has a left-hand thread, so you undo it the opposite way around (I wasted a couple of hours trying to figure that one out). Mate the plug and socket and while holding the locking collar tight with one hand, twist the cable grip clockwise (as viewed from the plug side) with the other hand.

Figure 4-6 shows a disassembled plug and the socket.

---

[2]If you want different number of poles, you'll find these Y2M series connectors go up to very large pin counts. Check out the Y2M-65TK!

Figure 4-6. *Disassembled plug and socket*

For the near-sensor connector, I just used a five-way DIN plug and bulkhead socket that I had handy (though it only needed to be a three-way plug, strictly speaking). The DC plug was a standard DC jack to match the 2.1 mm pin plug that the power supply came with. Examples of DC jacks come from

- www.sparkfun.com (sku: PRT-10785) (United States).

- www.maplin.co.uk (stock number JK09K) (UK).

Obviously, you should match the DC power jack that you use to the one that is already fitted to your +12V DC power supply. I'm afraid that DC power jacks are bit of a minefield because there are so many different pin sizes and barrel depths. I always find it best to take the one I am trying to match to the store and make sure it fits, there and then.

The power supply I used for my installation was just a 12V 3-amp unit that I got cheaply from an auction site. The project only needs 2 amps really, but this power supply (originally made for a flat-screen computer monitor) was brand new, unused, and very cheap. It works really well. You may already have something similar that you could use, but if not, a suitable power supply should not be hard to find at a good price.

Having settled on the connectors and drawn up the final circuit diagram and connection schedule I got busy putting it all together. Figures 4-7 and 4-8 show the final circuit diagram, with connector details and a pictorial view of the connections and installation layout. These are only provided as examples as, should you decide to build something like this for yourself, you will probably have to vary the details to fit your installation, your requirements, and the connectors you use.

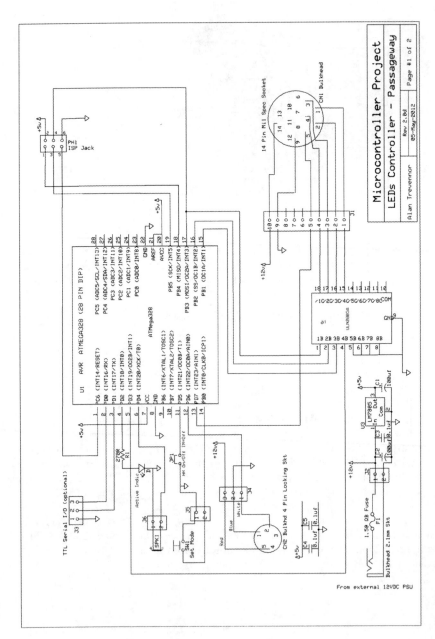

Figure 4-7. Circuit Diagram

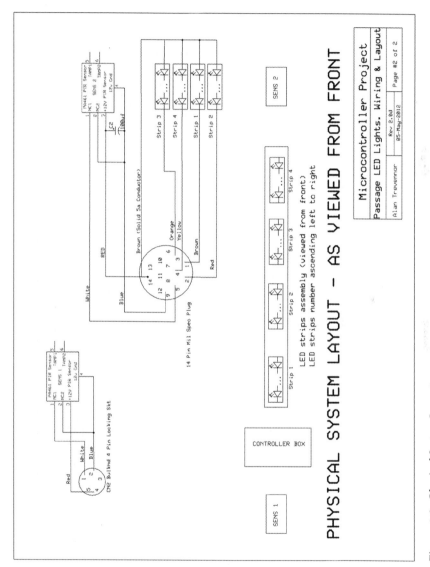

Figure 4-8. Physical System Layout

The following summarizes points of interest in these diagrams:

- In the finished version, the ISP connector is now a six-way ISP connector consisting of two rows of three pins, not the breakout board that was used for prototyping on the test rig. This should be made with two rows of three header pins.

  See Chapter 2 of *Practical AVR Microcontrollers* (Apress, 2012) for an explanation of ISP programming. Adding an ISP connector to this project makes it possible to update the controller's software in situ, using your Pololu (or any other) ISP programmer. When viewed from the topside, this connector should be wired to look like Figure 4-9.

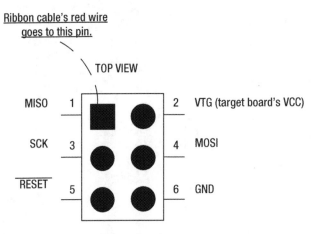

Figure 4-9. *ISP connector details*

- Note that, in this final version of the hardware design, the +5V regulator and associated capacitors have been added to allow the +5V supply to be derived from the +12V input.

- The +12V DC power supply coming in via the DC jack passes through a plastic cased inline fuse holder–inside the control box–before getting onto the board through a screw connector.

- The serial lines (TX, RX, and ground) are brought out to a three-way miniature screw connector. The signals from the near sensor (sensor 1) are also brought onto the board via a three-way screw connector.

- The signals coming in from the 14-pin mil socket are carried through to the board using a ten-way header pin strip and socket.

- The piezo electric speaker is held onto the side of the control box by two small bolts (see Figure 4-14). This results in a maximum loudness from it. You could drill a cluster of small holes in the box side to let more sound out, as I did, but I didn't find that made much difference in the end.

Figures 4-10 through 4-16 show photos of the various built pieces and the finished result.

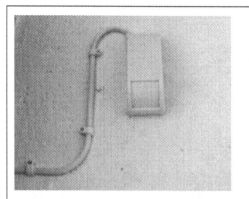

Figure 4-10. *The far sensor (sensor 2) installed*

The sensors were both installed by fixing them to the wall with a small screw. Six-core alarm wire cable was used for the connections, though only three wires are used. The cable from the far-end sensor (pictured) was connected to the ribbon cable and +12V power supply inside the light holder assembly–as described earlier.

Figure 4-11. *The 12V DC power supply*

The power unit was hidden away in a space under the stairs. A small hole through the wall allowed the DC side of the power supply (exiting left in this photo) to get to the control box (see below in this photo sequence).

Note: It is *very important* to make sure with an "always on" project like this to correctly fuse the mains supply side of the power supply. In this case I was able to get a qualified electrician to fit a fused switch box in the mains path to this PSU. But, whatever the arrangement used, it is absolutely necessary to make sure that a low-amp fuse (3 amps at most) is in the mains path. Any malfunction in the PSU will simply then blow the fuse, maintaining your safety.

Figure 4-12. *The built control box (view 1)*

The box used was a plastic project box measuring about 5" x 3" (127 mm × 76 mm); holes were cut out of the sides for the 14-way connector, the DIN connector, the DC jack, and the push button (the button is shown in this photo at top right)

The circuit was built up on a piece of tripad solder board which was then mounted on spacers into the box.

Figure 4-13. *The built control box (view 2)*

The second view of the internals of the control box shows the connector mounts in more detail. The 14-way military connector is at left, then comes the DC jack for power, then the DIN connector used to connect the near sensor (sensor 1).

Figure 4-14. *Detail showing the piezo mount*

This photo shows details of how the piezo speaker is mounted. Two nuts and bolts through the side of the box hold it captive by its edges. It needs to be able to flex in the middle to make the maximum volume of sound.

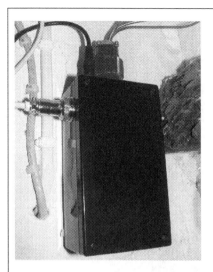

Figure 4-15. The control box, installed

This photo shows the control box installed high up, close to ceiling level.

The DIN plug at left is bringing in the signals from the near sensor. The DC power plug is top left —coming in from the understair location shown earlier. The 14-way mil connector at top center provides connections to the light holder assembly and–via that–to the far sensor.

Figure 4-16. Light exit, cut into wire channel

Close up on one of the light exits that are cut in the underside in the wire channel. These have to be approximately the same length as the light emitting portion of the LED strips used.

Figure 4-17 shows the lights all on, having just faded up in sequence–triggered by my approach.

Figure 4-17. The finished effect

I might even get rid of that pendant light now!

Waterfall Lights Mark II

It's always the way that, a while after something is made, you start second-guessing the design, the approach, the details–everything! In this case I haven't torn it out and started again (yet) because the original works well and fills the need nicely. However, although the four-LED string version is very pretty, it's not the waterfall I originally envisaged. So, I couldn't help wondering how easy it would be to do the project a different way . . . so I have done a design for a Mark II version that uses more LEDs in smaller groups. It's just a design, but here it is!

Mark II Electronics

As you may remember, the reason that the first version ended up with four LED strips, rather than the six or eight I had originally envisaged, was that the ATmega328 (and in fact all of that series of AVRs), when used with the Arduino software, only offers four PWM outputs with rock-solid reliability. There are two others, but their PWM outputs are subject to contention with timer functions of the Arduino software which results in unreliable turn-offs and consequent possible timing problems. I also experimented with the softPWM library that is available from

`http://code.google.com/p/rogue-code/wiki/SoftPWMLibraryDocumentation`

That library allows you to use up to 16 pins as PWM outputs. However, although the library works fine with just a small main loop, when I added my code, I ran into problems. After a lot of head scratching and Googling, I was forced to the conclusion that something my code was doing was occasionally sabotaging the library code, making it do very sudden or jerky fades or just stopping altogether for seconds at a time. Just running the demo version alone was fine, but when I added my code, something to do with the timer functions I need to use was causing problems. It's likely that someone with a deeper knowledge of the Arduino software than myself could resolve this, but I ran out of time and patience.

In the first version, I also needed to use a driver chip to drive the LED strips since the AVR cannot do this directly.

For the MKII version design I briefly considered using a chip called the M5450–which is a 34 output LED driver that has a serial input. The problem was that the M5450 does not do PWM, which I really wanted to keep in the picture. However, I clearly had to abandon the idea of using PWM direct from the AVR.

Then, a chip called the TLC5940 caught my eye. This chip (from Texas Instruments) offers the following facilities:

- 16 outputs–all offering PWM at 4096 different levels (much finer control than the 256 levels offered by the Arduino PWM).

- One common input sets the output current limit for all 16 outputs. This prevents outputs going over-current if there is a fault condition and protects the chip against damage.

- Each of the 16 outputs can (in theory) supply up to 120 milliamps–though it's not clear whether you could use all outputs at that full amperage for very long without the chip shutting down due to an over-temperature error.

- The data specifying the brightness value for the 16 outputs is sent via a serial data transfer from the MCU to the TLC5940 using just four wires. Data can be sent at 30 MHz, which I think means that you could change the intensity of all 16 outputs around 150,000 times per second if your MCU could feed them that fast. Easily fast enough for a little bit of gentle fading in and out anyway.

- Various extra features such as slightly staggered LED turn-on times to minimize current inrush problems for the power supply, a facility to detect failed LEDs, a thermal error flag, and so on.

- Texas seems to have designed this chip with large-scale uses in mind. If you were building up a large matrix of LEDs as pixels in a picture or graphics display (such as you might see in a stadium or public mall) you would probably be very concerned about even quite small differences in the brightness of individual LEDs within your display. Using PWM techniques does tend to heighten such differences. So, if you're trying to build up a picture on a LED matrix and you can't precisely control each pixel, then you will have problems. Therefore, the other major functional block of the TLC5940 is a dot correction EEPROM which allows you to make and store a PWM correction factor for each output so that you can exactly match the output to the individual LED that is connected to it. In our application this whole area is of little interest to us, since we are using the LEDs as lighting, not as picture elements: so, we leave that block of functionality disabled. Be aware that if you did want to use this side of the chip, you would need a +22V "programming voltage" to be able to reprogram the intensity correction EEPROM.

- The ability to cascade devices. If 16 outputs is not enough, you connect two or more TLC5940s in series and you can add sets of 16 lights, so start with 16 then go to 32, 48, 64–or whatever.

This one chip could solve the PWM problem with the first design and also eliminate the need to use the ULN2803A that was required for the first version. If you're thinking of getting one of these to try out on a breadboard, make sure you order the TLC5940NT– where the NT denotes the DIP package: The device is also available in a couple of surface-mount packagings which you won't be able to use on the breadboard.

Full details of the TLC5940 can of course be seen in its data sheet; go grab a copy from

www.ti.com/lit/ds/symlink/tlc5940.pdf

However, be warned, it's not the most approachable piece of technical documentation you're ever going to read! In fact, lucky for us, that doesn't matter. Alex Leone has created an Arduino library to take most of the pain out of driving the TLC5940 for us. See details and download information at

http://code.google.com/p/tlc5940arduino/
http://alex.kathack.com/codes/tlc5940arduino/html_r014/

When using this library, you connect your AVR to the TLC5940 using the pins that the library requires, or you can try using other pins if you prefer. The file tlc_config.h is where you can make those changes. See the "files" tab on the second of the web sites mentioned previously. The library comes with numerous example programs. Using this library you can cascade up to 16 chips, giving a possible total of 256 individual LEDs or clusters of LEDs. If you're prepared to go in for a little LED multiplexing, then you can use TLC5940s to control an enormous number of LEDs.

The installation documentation tells you to install the library into the libraries subfolder of your Arduino sketchbook folder. However, I found that when I did that (on Windows or Linux) that I got compile errors when I tried to use even the demo programs; this was under Arduino release 0.22.

However, when I installed the library into the main installation hierarchy it all worked fine. Since the library was created in 2010, it might be that subsequent Arduino updates have created this problem, but anyway the fix for this, if you do get the problem, is to install in the library subfolder that you will find under your installation location: on Windows XP it's

```
C:\Program Files\Arduino-xxx
```

where xxx is the Arduino version number. Under the installation location you will find a folder called libraries which is where you should install the TLC library, in its own subfolder. On Vista and Windows 7 you will need to have administrator privileges to do this installation. It's not a problem on Windows XP or earlier.

On Linux and on Mac OS X you'll find the base directory for Arduino at

```
/usr/share/Arduino
```

Under the installation location, you will find a directory called library and you should install the TLC library there under its own subdirectory. On Linux or Mac machines you will need to use the sudo command or login as the superuser to acquire the privileges required to do this installation.

If your Arduino installation is, for some reason, nonstandard and you can't find the Arduino software set, a simple trick is to look at the properties of the clickable link that you usually use to run Arduino. Those properties should show you where the software was installed.

The downside of having to install the library under the installation folder is that, when you upgrade your Arduino software, if the old version is removed, you will also lose any custom libraries you have installed in this way. Therefore, keep copies of downloaded libraries somewhere safe, so that you can reinstate them after future upgrades if need be.

So, an MKII design using the TLC5940 would have a lot of possibilities. It would be possible (although an absolute wiring nightmare) to use a large number of individual LEDs and to have them fade one at a time. Or, we could use 5050 series RGB LED strips, and use multiple TLC5940s to drive them in various different sexy ways. The temptation to go overboard is very great. If we were we creating a disco light show or something of that kind, those would be very good options, but with our feet firmly on the ground we have to repeat the calming mantra "Passageway Lights" over and over again.

Take-Two Circuit Diagram

In the end, I decided to stay with a relatively simple scheme of up to 16 single-color LED strips, with the ability in the software to use as many or as few of the 16 as required. Figure 4-18 shows the circuit diagram.

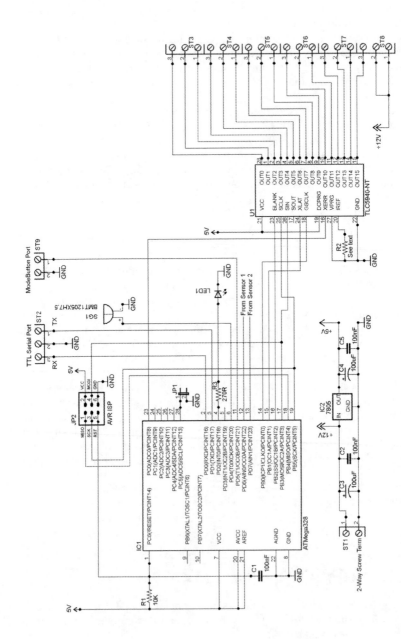

Figure 4-18. *Mark 2a passage lights circuit diagram*

In this circuit diagram (intended to be built up as a stand-alone project, not a test rig project) the default pins, as specified in the TLC5490 library, drive the device. Most of the other peripherals from the previous iteration (the tone sounder, the mode switch, the sensors) connect via the same pins as before: the exception is the jumper, which now connects via Arduino's pin A5 (pin 28). Note also that the XERR pin of the TLC5940 is connected to A0 of the AVR (pin 23) this gives you the possibility of checking every now and again as to whether the 5940 has detected any LED errors.

The 5940's outputs are extended out to miniature screw connectors. You would connect each set of LED strips with its positive lead to one of the +12V leads and its other to whatever output of the 5940 you needed.

R2 on this diagram is connected to the IREF pin of the TLC5940. This pin is used to set the maximum current output that can be drawn from each of the output pins. You connect the pin to ground through a resistor and the current it pulls is used to determine the current limit the chip will apply to each of the outputs. The value of the resistor is determined by the following formula:

$$R = (1.24 / Imax) \times 31.5$$

For example, if you want the max current to be 80 milliamps (0.080 amps) this becomes

$$(1.24 / 0.080) \times 31.5 = 488.25$$

So, in such a case you would probably use the nearest preferred resistor value, which is 470 Ohms.

The TLC5940NT needs a constant frequency square wave into its Grayscale Clock (GSCLK) input on pin 18. This signal is used as the master reference clock for all of the chip's PWM operations. In the default hardware configuration, instanced by the TLC5940 library, the AVR's pin 5 (Arduino pin D3) is set to give out a constant PWM pulse (at about 500 Hz) to provide this, and that arrangement will work well. However, rather than sticking with that, I perversely decided to extend out the AVR's 8 MHz clock, just to see if would work–and it does!

The AVR ATMEGA328 has a feature whereby its system clock can be extended out to pin 14 (Arduino digital pin 8). When used in this mode, the AVR calls this pin CKOUT; if you program the CKOUT fuse, whatever clock the AVR is using is enabled to be output on the CKOUT pin. This applies whether you are using the internal 8 MHz clock (as we are) or an external crystal–as detailed in Chapter 3 of *Practical AVR Microcontrollers* (Apress, 2012). This CKOUT feature allows you to use the same clock frequency for all devices in your project. In this case it's the TLC5940.

To extend out the AVR's internal clock, we use AVRDude (see Chapter 3 of *Practical AVR Microcontrollers* [Apress, 2012] for extensive details and examples of using this useful program) to reprogram the fuse bit. So, how do we use AVRDude to program the AVR chip to activate CKOUT? Well, as we saw in Chapter 3, the format of the FLB is

FuseName	CKDIV8	CKOUT	SUT1	SUT0	CKSEL3	CKSEL2	CKSEL1	CKSEL0
Bit #	7	6	5	4	3	2	1	0

So, in this context, bit 6 is the one of interest. We start by using AVRDude to find out the current value of the fuse. Assuming that the fuse is at its default state, we will need to invert it to turn on CKOUT.

▓ **Tip** In the following command sequence you will have to "plug in" your own comms port (e.g., COM2 or /dev/ttyACM0). You will have to change the DESTination to CON for Windows or "-" (meaning standard output) for Unix. If you are not using an ATmega328p chip but some other AVR variant (e.g., an ATmega328), you will have to change that value too. See the section "AVRDude" in Chapter 3 of *Practical AVR Microcontrollers* (Apress, 2012) for lots more details on these areas.

Begin by opening a command (terminal) window on the desktop machine to which your AVR and programmer are connected.

Now, make sure AVRDude can "see" your AVR chip.

```
avrdude -p m328p -c avrisp2 -P {YOUR_COM_PORT}.
```

This should make AVRDude print out the signature bytes of your AVR and make it verify the fuses. Next, make AVRDude show you the current lower fuse byte value

```
avrdude -p m328p -c avrisp2 -P {YOUR COM PORT} -U lfuse:r:DEST:h.
```

This will show you—in hexadecimal format—the current value of the lower fuse byte. You can decode it using the bit layout diagram shown previously; or, if you prefer, you can use the online fusecalc site at

```
www.engbedded.com/fusecalc
```

to do it for you. On that site you enter your AVR part number, or use the nearest one to it, if you can't find the precise one (e.g., if you have an ATmega168-P just use ATmega168). Then, enter the value returned by AVRDude into the LFUSE box near the bottom of the calculator and you will see the tick boxes change to the settings represented by the code you just entered. Change the value of CKOUT using the tick box and you will then see the new value you need to program.

Remember that a "programmed" (active) bit in an AVR fuse is read by AVRDude as 0 and an unprogrammed (inactive) bit will read as a 1. This is the opposite way round to most logic systems. So, suppose that AVRDude returned the value xE2 (assuming you unprogrammed CKDIV8–bit 7–earlier in the book to get your MCU running at 8 MHz) you would just need to invert bit 6 and make that into xA2. In other words:

Bit #	7	6	5	4	3	2	1	0
Bin	1	1	1	0	0	0	1	0
HEX	E				2			

Becomes

Bit #	7	6	5	4	3	2	1	0
Bin	1	0	1	0	0	0	1	0
HEX	A				2			

We program the required value into the fuses, using the command

```
avrdude -p m328p -c avrisp2 -P {YOUR COM PORT} -U lfuse:w:0xA2:m.
```

And that's it! You should have a steady square wave clock coming out of what is now the CKOUT pin of your MCU. This technique is useful over and over again in designing MCU projects because it saves you having to provide separate circuitry for clocks to other devices–which usually means adding extra devices onto an already crowded board.

As of this writing the MKII project is just a proof of concept on a breadboard, and it seems to work okay there just using individual LEDs as proxies for LED strips, though for some reason that I don't understand I did have to reduce the IREF resistor lower than the equation suggested to get a good brightness. I've done a rough and ready conversion of the software for the MKII which is available through the book's web site (www.apress.com/9781430244462).

As a final word, the diagram in Figure 4-19 shows how you connect up two TLC5940s in a chain to give yourself more than 16 outputs. This is not a full waterfall lights diagram; it just shows you how to chain up your TLCs! Don't forget that, to use a circuit like this with two TLC5940s, you will need to edit the file tlc_config.h to change the value of NUM_TLCS. As stated earlier, you'll find that file in the same folder as the other TLC5940 library components.

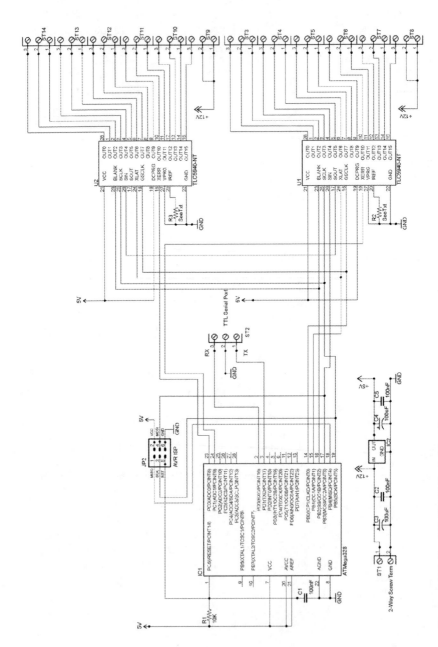

Figure 4-19. Dual TLC5940 Basic Circuit

Summary

In this chapter we have looked in detail at how to build a useful home lighting project–one with several novel features. We have looked at some different options for how to make it and some possible alternative electronic approaches. We've also seen how an MCU subsystem can gain the ability to respond to external commands. In this way, something that might once have been simply a standalone item, could in fact–with the proper infrastructure provided–participate in a wider, more coheseive whole-home control system.

Coming Up Next

Project 5: Moving to Mesmerize.

CHAPTER 5

Moving to Mesmerize

In this chapter we'll look at three small projects and some associated ideas and techniques. Each project involves actual or virtual movement. Each of these projects is–while simple in itself–intended to provide some interest and provoke other ideas, or just provide a little simple fun for you or whoever you feel like sharing it with.

Duck Shooter Game

Duck Shooter is a classic game that you've probably played at the fairground or arcade. In those real-world versions of the game, hinged cartoon duck targets go around on a chain and you have to use the provided air guns to try to hit them as they move across your line of sight. If you get all the ducks down before your time is up, you get a prize (usually quite a perfunctory one).

There have been duck shooter arcade games, pinball games, and alley games since the late 1930s. Ever since computer games were new, versions of this game have been available. For example, Sega had a version of it in 1975, various versions of the game have appeared over the years which use TTL or CMOS logic chips, and of course in more recent years there have been numerous MCU implementations and numerous Java game implementations of the same basic game. Well, you'll be glad to hear that although the format of this game follows the duck shoot format, there isn't a duck in sight. They're LEDs really, but we'll call them ducks. Okay then!

Following is a summary of the rules:

- You have an 11-slot "duck run"; each slot is represented by an LED.

- You have a button to press that represents your gun. Your gun is locked into position and can only shoot at the middle slot of the duck run, represented by LED number 6.

- At the start of each level in the game, a single duck (represented by a lit LED) progresses across the duck run from left to right. When it reaches the end, it reappears at the left and starts again.

- You must time your shot so that you hit the duck when it reaches the center slot. If you do it right, you hit the duck and its light fades out. If you miss, the duck is cloned! So now there are two ducks parading around in front of you. Miss again and there'll be three ducks–and so on. When you fire your gun, the duck run stops for a moment, so you can see what's happening.

- When you have managed to kill off all the ducks, the level ends and you move on to the next one. Each level is the same, except the duck's progress gets faster and faster and that means that you have to be more and more precise.

- If you manage to play through all the levels your reward is . . . a little light show on the duck run. It's a perfunctory prize, just like at the fairground. How true to life is that?

In hardware terms, this is quite a simple game. Eleven LEDs are connected from the +5-volt supply, via 11 270 ohm resistors to 11 AVR pins. A push button is connected to a twelfth AVR pin. And that's it really!

▓ **Note**   We'll also build in a secret Easter egg feature; when the player presses the gun button for more than ten seconds, the game will show a preview of the winner's light show.

The Duck Shooter Circuit

Figure 5-1 shows the circuit diagram. In the diagram, I have instanced a push button with a built-in LED (S2-LED), but you don't have to use such a push button. I just used a little PCB-mounted push button on my prototype (as we shall see later). An illuminated push button is just for show really, but it would look nice!

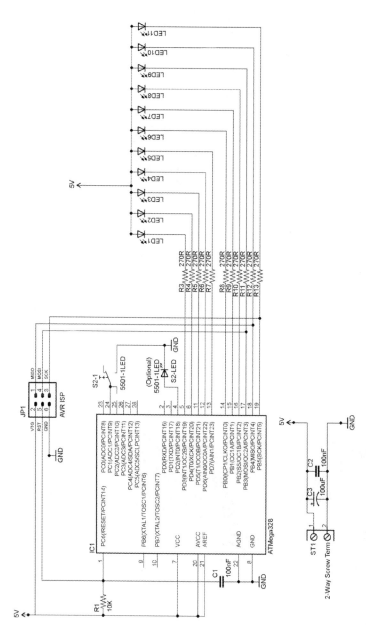

***Figure 5-1.** Duck Shooter game circuit diagram*

I'm going to use this project to show how to transfer a design from a breadboard to something more permanent. It's not an overly complex design, but it is complex enough to show you how to make the transfer from breadboard to solder board.

Making Duck Shooter into a Keeper

All electronics enthusiasts have their own favorite way of producing a "keeper" project (i.e., one they want to keep, not just a breadboard version that they subsequently break up). Some favor making a printed circuit board (or using services allied to open source packages like Fritzing or Eagle to get a PCB produced for them); some favor a strip board on which they solder their components and cut away sections of copper strip to isolate them from one another; some people like using protoboards, where they solder their components into individual holes and then solder on wires from point to point; some people use various kinds of wire-wrap schemes. For a selection of different solder boards see the following link:

`www.verotl.com/prototyping-products`

My own favorite for simpler keeper projects is tri-pad solder strip board. This simplifies the tedious business of cutting off copper connections between components because, on a tripad board there are only ever three holes connected to any one connection point—thus the name. For an example product, see

- `www.maplin.co.uk` (UK) (stock number JP52G).

I haven't found a U.S. source of this product, though I'm sure there must be one, but you could use various protoboards.

- `www.mouser.com` (stock number 574-45P80-1).

- `www.sparkfun.com` (stock number PRT-08619).

Figure 5-2 shows a close-up of a tripad board.

Figure 5-2. *Close-up of a tripad board*

As you can see, the solder pads are arranged in groups of three pads (thus the name), so you just need to choose your component positions such that they bridge across tripad islands and then you can make other connections from there. There is no tedious track cutting required–as when you use continuous solder strip boards–but you can still get a useful number of components on quite a small board space. The holes are 0.1" (2.54 mm) apart and for the Duck Shooter game we need a board that is 33 holes by 38 holes (give or take one or two either way). This makes the board dimensions about 3.5" × 3.75" (850 mm × 952 mm).

Building Duck Shooter

Figure 5-3 shows a piece of tripad board cut to size and with some mounting holes drilled through it, one near each corner. Drill carefully and slowly and hold the board steady; it's very easy to break off a corner if the drill catches because you go too fast. Been there, done that!

Figure 5-3. *Tripad board cut to size for Duck Shooter game*

I'm a fan of IC (integrated circuit) sockets; some people don't like them, but I've found that they save a lot of hassle if in the future you need to change a chip out. Yes, after some period of time (usually years) they can cause connection problems due to contact oxidization; however, such problems are easily fixed by reseating the chip in its socket. Also, using sockets means that you don't have to expose your chips to soldering heat, since you solder the socket into place and plug the chip in later on. So, I almost always use sockets–as you can see from the picture of the completed topside of the Duck Shooter board in Figure 5-4.

Figure 5-4. *Duck Shooter project board topside*

As the photo shows, the LEDs are arranged across the board at three-hole intervals. The button is at the opposite end of the board. The MCU is in the middle, and ISP jack is close to it. The power connector is at the top of the board above the LEDS. Before installing any wiring jumpers or resistors on the board, I used a Sharpie pen to make a bold line from the button to the target center LED, indicating the line of fire.

It's not strictly required (and it's not on the circuit diagram) but since I had an old IC socket, I cut a couple of pin sections from it to install a socket arrangement for pins 2 and 3 (serial RX and TX, respectively) in case I needed them. The software for this game does output some game metrics to the serial port, which might be of interest to someone . . . sometime! Figure 5-5 shows the serial port and the ISP plug for programming the MCU *in situ*.

Figure 5-5. *ISP -plug and serial port add-on wire socket*

Most of the wires for the ISP plug (and a few other wires) are actually routed under the board as you can perhaps tell from the photo in Figure 5-6. For details about the ISP connector, refer to the "About In-System Programming" section of Chapter 2 of *Practical AVR Microcontrollers* (Apress, 2012), specifically Figure 2-9.

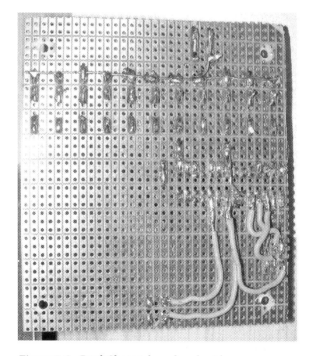

Figure 5-6. *Duck Shooter board underside*

You may just be able to see in Figure 5-6 the line of stiff wire that goes from left to right along the + side of all the LEDs. This carries the +5V feed to the LEDs.

If you've never made a board like this before it can seem quite a daunting task. However, the reality is that as long as you have the right tools for the job and some patience, it's not hard. It's just a question of methodically working through it and not rushing it. Your fine-tip soldering iron, your helping-hands gripper, and your magnifying glass should all help make it easier and even enjoyable. Use the solid wire–similar to the breadboard jumper wire–which, by now, you should be used to using. Avoid using stranded wire, which tends to "feather" at the ends and make hard-to-spot short circuits between components.

Following are some tips and points to watch out for:

- If you are unfamiliar with soldering, find one of the many tutorials on the Internet before you begin. The golden rule (as you will see in any of those tutorials) is "heat the job, not the solder." In other words, if you're soldering the pin of an LED, heat up the pin and then apply the solder to the pin: don't heat the solder and let the melted solder fall onto the pin! The latter method will make what is known as a "dry joint" which–in a digital circuit–may initially work but will soon fail. Heat the job, not the solder. Did I say that before? Good! It's very important.

- Be safety aware: if you have some safety glasses that give you good visibility, use them. Never, ever, flick solder around. Hot solder burns, and burns and burns. It burns holes in carpets, furniture, and, given half a chance, *you*. Don't give it *any* chance. Use a soldering iron with a proper holder or holster.

- Inhale as little solder smoke as possible. If you have a desk fan around, run it on low to waft the smoke away from you toward an open window if at all possible. If the room has an extractor fan, use it. Don't solder in a confined space. In any case, find a way to avoid breathing in any significant amount of solder smoke.

- Be methodical. Work from the circuit diagram (or a photo copy of it) and as you install each component or wire, cross it off on the diagram. Use a pencil so that you can erase any mistakes you make.

- Don't solder one point for too long. Even things like resistors and capacitors can be damaged if exposed to the heat of a soldering iron for too long. ICs, transistors, LEDs, and other semiconductor devices are very easily heat damaged, so don't hold the soldering iron tip on their leads for more than two or three seconds.

- Where two adjacent pins need to be connected, don't bother putting a wire between them, heat *both* pins and flood that little area with solder until they are joined together by a solder blob.

- Keep the soldering iron tip reasonably clean. Use a piece of kitchen paper towel which has been dampened with a little water to wipe the tip with if it gets messy. After cleaning, melt a little solder onto the tip to keep it coated. Many soldering stations (usually consisting of the iron itself and a holder or holster) will come with a cloth or special sponge that you can moisten with a little water. You then use this dampened surface for cleaning the soldering tip.

- When you have finished (or think you have–there's always one more thing to do!) go around the board with a watchmakers' fine-blade screwdriver or perhaps a craft knife and carefully run it between adjacent pins that are not meant to be connected to make sure there are no minute solder bridges shorting them together.

- When you connect your power source, make sure you have a fuse in the + lead. See the "A +5-Volt Regulated Supply" section in Chapter 2 of *Practical AVR Microcontrollers* (Apress, 2012) for information on how to do this if you are in any doubt. The Duck Shooter game uses no more than 1 amp, so a fuse at that value should be sensitive enough. If you're using a bench supply that has a current limiter, make sure the current limiter is set on low for the first power-up of any new board.

If you are truly daunted by the prospect of building this as your first soldering project, try an easier "get started" project to cut your teeth on. A good project for this might be one of the 555 timer chip circuits shown in Chapter 3 of *Practical AVR Microcontrollers* (Apress, 2012). That might give you the confidence to progress to this one. Like most things, it does get easier, the more you do it!

As the circuit diagram shows, the Duck Shooter game is intended to run from a +5V supply. However, you could also run it from 3 x AA batteries (giving about 4.5V) if you wanted to. The LEDs won't be quite as bright, but the difference is very small.

Going Further

Many developments of the basic game presented here are possible. You may want to build your version into a project box of some kind, or even build it into something else. A friend suggested it might be fun to build it into the arm of a chair in a TV room. I guess it would give you something to do during those interminable commercial breaks! If you wanted to box the project, you would need to raise up the LEDs above the rest of the circuit, either by leaving their legs longer than I have done on my prototype or perhaps by using bits of socket strips (like the one I added on for the serial port) to raise up the level of the LEDs. For a compact version of the game you could use bar graph LEDs such as

- www.sparkfun.com (sku: com-09935) (United States).

- www.maplin.co.uk (stock number BT65V) (UK).

The problem is, those only come in ten-LED groups (you can also get eight-way groups if you shop around), and so you'd have to rearrange the game somehow.

If you wanted to go nuts on the game you could dispense with the idea of driving the LEDs from the AVR directly. You could use a smaller AVR and one or more TLC5940 chips (see Chapter 4) to drive a much larger number of LEDs which you could arrange in various shapes (circles, circuits, etc.).

Duck Shooter Software

The Duck Shooter game software is quite big and so is not reproduced in full in the book itself, but you can download it via the book's web site (www.apress.com/9781430244462). The following is a code walk, function by function:

Function Name	Commentary
Declarations	The declarations section consists of numerous #define directives to define constants for the program. Notable are the declarations for LOW_LED and HIGH_LED which define the lowest and highest numbered Arduino port pins used for the required 11 LEDs. You can change these if you want, but the program assumes throughout that the LED pins are in a contiguous block.
	Also worthy of note is the SPEED_STEP variable which controls the amount of speed increase that happens between each level of the game. If you make this value larger, the higher levels of the game won't be quite so fast.
	Note that the circuit diagram and the code (via GUN_BUTTON_LED) provide for the possibility of a button with an integral LED. If you don't use such a thing and prefer to just use a standard, unlit push button as I did, then it doesn't matter, but the provision exists.
	Finally for this section, note the Debug definition. If you declare this as true then the program will output extra information to the serial channel (which you don't have to use–there is no serial input required for this project, so the serial channel is completely optional) and the embedded Easter egg is enabled. This latter feature means you can see the "winner's" light show by holding down the button for more than ten seconds.
	An important feature of my implementation of this game is the way the animation is done. An in-memory representation of the state of each LED is held in a 16-bit variable called ducks, in which the lower 11 bits each correspond to one of the LEDs. Functions that want to alter the state of the LEDs alter bits in ducks rather than directly writing to the LEDs. Each time through the main loop of the program, the state of the duck animation is advanced by one place, based on the content of ducks. In this way, only one function touches the hardware in the main loop. However, many other functions–those that run when the main game is not active–such as the showSpeedLevel function and the winner's light show, do directly output to the LED pins because the normal game animation is suspended while those things are running anyway.

(continued)

Function Name	Commentary
setup()	The setup() function contains a useful map that relates LEDs to pins and bits within the ducks variable.
	The gun button input and LED pins are defined and initialized. We're using what Arduino calls input pin A1 for our button input, but we're using it as a digital pin–not analog at all. We enable a pull-up on this port pin so we don't need an external pull-up resistor. Next, the LED pins are all initialized to be outputs. Finally we reset the ducks to their default value, which is one LED on and the rest off. We show the speed level and then we initialize the serial channel.
loop()	In the main loop, we read the button to see if it's pressed. If it is pressed
	• We start the clock, so that when it has been released we will know how long it was pressed for.
	• We advance the state of the gun LED flashing (if it's in use)
	• We invert the state of the firing line LED, updating the ducks variable (described above) in the light of whether the user missed or hit a duck. If the user hit a duck then the target LED fades out (the duck dies!) if he or she missed, then the firing line LED fades up into life (an extra duck is born).
	If the user did hit a duck and we faded it out, we check to see whether that was the last duck. If it was, then the level is over with and we do the things we need to do to bring on the next level of the game.
	We wait for the button to be released and see how long it was pressed for. If it was pressed for more than ten seconds, we do the hidden Easter egg feature.
	If the button was pressed normally (i.e., not to get the cheat) or it was not pressed at all, then we're still playing and we call the animLeds() function which is described later.
showSpeedLevel()	Speed level and game level are the same thing. This function (intended to be used to introduce a new game level) flashes the LEDs a few times (using direct LED access) and then puts all the LEDs on, and then pares them down to the point where they show the new game level (i.e., four LEDS on for level 4). After a short wait, all LEDs go off and the game resumes at the new level.
turnAllLedsOn(dly) turnAllLedsOff(dly)	These two functions turn all the LEDs on or off in sequence at the speed indicated in their argument dly.

(continued)

Function Name	Commentary
flashAlternates(dly, altCycles, varyTiming)	This function flashes the two groups of LED on either side of the firing line alternately. It does the specified number of cycles, with dly setting the speed and with a random element if indicated in the varyTiming Boolean variable. This function is used as part of the winner's light show display.
setGunButtonLedState (newState)	Sets the gun button's LED state. Used when there is an appropriate device in use.
doGblFlash()	Inverts the state of the gun button's LED, if in use.
animLeds(dValue)	Advances the state of the LED's animation by one tick. Incorporates a delay – dValue. This value is used to cause the animation function to block for a short time, thus limiting how often it can be called. This function is where the contents of the ducks variable are made real by being written out to the hardware.
weHaveAWinner()	Does the winner's light show.
resetDucks()	Initializes the ducks variable that holds all the duck states. One duck is on; the rest are off.
doFadeOutLed(pinNum)	Using software PWM, this fades out the indicated LED. If the LED pinNum is sent as zero, then we fade out *all* the LEDs.
doEndTogetherLeds (iterations, stepTime)	This function is used by the winner's light show. It starts a single LED from each end and they progress to the middle where they meet and disappear. Iterations tell how many times to run it, and stepTime controls the speed.

And that's it for the Duck Shooter game. I hope you enjoy building and playing it.

MCU Shadow Puppets

The second of our simple projects in this chapter is somewhat grandiosely called an animation projector–but it's really just a simple MCU controller version of a shadow puppet. The idea is that a single strong light source in a darkened room can, when interrupted by a shape, cause that shape to appear enlarged on a screen or an opposite wall. If the shape moves across the light source, then you get the illusion of a large moving object on the wall opposite the apparatus. We've all played with this idea at some time or another.

In this project we set up a single bright light source (a high-intensity LED light) and we build a simple motorized movement mechanism using a servo motor and a few household bits and pieces to move a shape around in front of the light. In a darkened or low-lighted room it's very effective. We give the MCU the ability to control the light source and to move the shape and we can even allow the MCU to be commanded via the serial port, which would make it easier for this little project to form part of something larger, such as a coordinated display or an art installation using many such mechanisms, synchronized by a central controller.

Building the Shadow Puppets

To build this quickie project I used some bits of scrap wood, a few self-tapping screws, a strip of 1/4" (about 6 mm) plastic that I cut out of an old storage box that was out for recycling, some stiff wire, a rubber band, and a couple of hooks with self-tapping screws. I used a servo motor and 3W high-intensity LED. I only intended this as a proof of concept, not a "keeper" project.

First the servo motor is mounted on a frame made of scrap bits of wood, as you can see in Figure 5-7. Then, I drilled a pilot hole in one end of the frame and screwed one of the hooks into it. These don't have to be hooks; they could be long wood screws. Next, I drilled a hole in each end of the plastic strip and fixed the rubber band through one end: the other end of the rubber band goes around the hook.

Figure 5-7. *MCU shadow puppet*

Figure 5-8. *Rubber band and end anchor hook*

At the other end of the plastic strip, I used a piece of stiff solderable wire to link the plastic strip to the motor horn, which has a self-tapping screw (supplied with the motor accessories kit). I soldered the wire ends together to keep them from coming undone.

As it is pulled back and forth, the plastic strip (to which we will fix a silhouette) wants to twist axially. To stop this, I fitted a second hook into the frame to hold the plastic strip roughly vertical (see Figure 5-9). The photo in Figure 5-10 shows the whole thing.

Figure 5-9. *Motor end linkage*

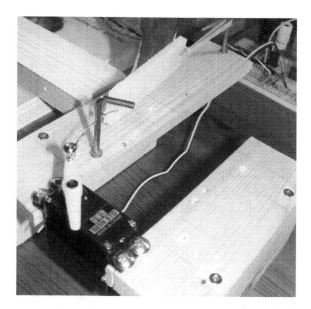

Figure 5-10. *Shadow puppet assembly complete*

Finally I used transparent tape to stick a silhouette to the plastic strip: since I can't draw to save my life, my wife kindly drew two sample silhouettes for me on 120 GSM paper. I had planned to mount these on cardboard once I had cut them out, but that proved unnecessary, the thick paper worked fine. In case you too are artistically challenged, I include these silhouettes (see Figure 5-11).

Figure 5-11. *Sample silhouettes by Wendy Trevennor*

The LED needs to be separate from the main frame so that its distance and height relative to the moving silhouette can be varied according to situation. So, I used some flat-head screws to fix it onto a couple of pieces of scrap stick wood that I made up into an L shape" as shown in Figure 5-12.

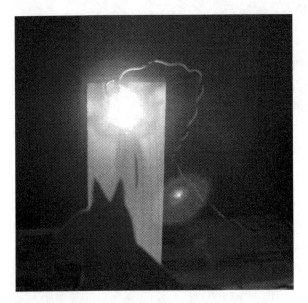

Figure 5-12. *LED shining on the silhouette*

When the whole thing is put together, with the room darkened and the software running (see Figure 5-13), the effect is really excellent.

Figure 5-13. *Big cat, little cat: the project running*

As you can see from the final picture in Figure 5-13, the silhouette size obtainable in a semidarkened room is quite impressive–it certainly impressed our real cat, which ran out of the room in a hurry. Of course, this is just a 3W LED; if you used a higher-power LED you could get an even better effect. I was so impressed by the results of this quickie project that I plan to build a more permanent version. I will use a 5- or 7-watt LED for the permanent version. The mechanism will use a reversible winding motor to get longer travel, and I will use a proper metal spring return instead of the rubber band.

The Shadow Puppet Circuit

The circuit diagram for this project is very simple (Figure 5-14). If you plan to build your own version of this as a keeper project, you'll need to build as per the circuit diagram.

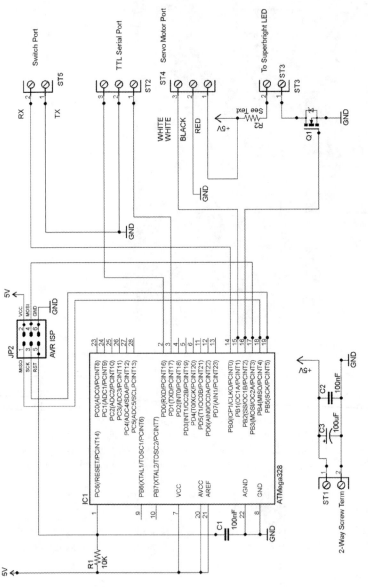

Figure 5-14. Shadow puppets circuit diagram

Referring to the circuit diagram you can see that this project only requires +5V, at about 1 amp–depending on which LED and motor you use. Because this project involves a motor (which can pull big startup currents for a brief instant) you will need to make sure the power supply rails have a good reservoir capacitor. You'll need at least a 100 uF capacitor across your +5V rail, 200 uF would be better! Without this, the motor might spike the power rail sufficiently enough to cause the MCU to crash or hang up. 100 uF proved sufficient for the motor I used, but if you, using a different motor, experience problems, try a larger value smoothing capacitor (or multiple 100 uF capacitors).

In this project, only three items are hung off the MCU: the switch, the servo motor, and the high-intensity LED.

The switch port (screw terminal 5, ST5) allows the connection of a push button to step the software through its different modes (see the "Shadow Puppets Software" section below). The ISP connector is the same as in the Duck Shooter project described earlier in this chapter.

The motor (attached via ST4) is a servo motor, as covered in Chapter 3 of *Practical AVR Microcontrollers* (Apress, 2012) and other places. This takes a direct logic connection from Arduino digital pin 9 (AVR pin 15). The servo motor is directly connected to the +5V supply lines and its control lead is connected to Arduino digital pin 9. We drive this in PWM mode in the software for this project.

There is a driver transistor for the high-power LED, and this hangs off Arduino digital pin 10 (AVR pin 16). Since the 3W LED that I used requires far more current than the AVR can directly supply to it, we have to use a driver transistor. I used a VNP10N6 MOSFET, which is a logic-level compatible MOSFET that includes a snubber diode. This device can sink up to 10 amps of current, so sinking 330 ma for our 3W high-intensity LED (or even a much more powerful one, should you choose to go down that route) is well within its capabilities. You could just as easily use some other logic-compatible MOSFET (e.g., an IRL540) in its place.

The MOSFET used here does not need a heatsink; it barely gets warm to the touch even after the LED has been on for half an hour. However, if you're using different components, remember to check for heat issues. The VNP10N6 MOSFET comes in a TO220 package, and the pinout (see diagram below) is a pretty standard one.

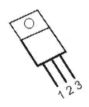

However, don't assume that *all* MOSFETs are connected like this, because although most of them are, there will be exceptions and if you make the wrong connections, you can all too easily damage your MOSFET and probably other components too. Always check the data sheet for your device to make sure you have the pinout right. For the VNP10N6 (and the IRL540), if you lay the component on its steel back, the three leads from it are as follows, from left to right:

- Terminal 1 is the input (gate).

- Terminal 2 is the drain (connect to the load): the metal tab is also connected to this terminal to aid in heatsinking.

- Terminal 3 is the source (connected to ground in this application).

The MOSFET connects to the screw terminals for the LED.

The serial port, although not used in the software as it stands, is extended out to ST2 so that it could be used with a TTL level serial port to receive commands if you wanted to extend the project for use in some larger scheme–as previously discussed.

The ISP connector is the same as in the Duck Shooter project described earlier in this chapter.

Shadow Puppets Software

The listing for the software for the shadow puppet project is quite short and reproduced in full here. There is nothing very complex about this software and I have commented it quite freely. The only thing that bears a little explanation is the program mode variable thisMode. Although it's an integer, in fact, we only care about the lowest weight two bits. Bit zero, if set, tells the program to power on the LED. Bit one, if set, tells the program to advance the motor position once each time through the main loop and to reset it when it has done a full sweep of the desired range. The following truth table summarizes the arrangement.

Bit 1	Bit 0	State selected
0	0	Motor and LED off
0	1	LED on. Motor off
1	0	LED off, motor on.
1	1	Both on.

```
/*

A sketch to control the simple shadow puppet rig
detailed in chapter 16 of "Practical AVR Microcontrollers".
The program runs in one of four modes:

00 = LED off, Motor Off
01 = LED on, Motor Off
02 = LED off, Motor On
03 = LED On, Motor On

When enabled, the motor sweeps back and forth to draw the
puppet across the light shone by the LED. This casts a moving
shadow on whatever surface the light hits (opposite wall etc).
*/

#define SWITCH_PIN 8
#define MOTOR_PIN 9
#define LED_PIN 10

#include <Servo.h>

Servo myMotor;    // The servo motor
int theAngle=0;   // Remembered angle of the motor.
int thisMode =0;  // Program's current mode.

void setup()
{
  myMotor.attach(MOTOR_PIN);      // Setup the motor control pin
  pinMode(LED_PIN,OUTPUT);        // Make the LED control pin an o/p
  pinMode(SWITCH_PIN,INPUT);      // Make the switch pin an input.
  digitalWrite(SWITCH_PIN,HIGH);  // Enable the pull up.

  digitalWrite(LED_PIN,LOW);      // Ensure the LED starts Off
  myMotor.write(0);               // Ensure the motor starts at home pos.

  Serial.begin(9600);             // Init serial - minimal use.
}

void loop()
{
  // Is the switch pressed?
  if (digitalRead(SWITCH_PIN) == LOW)
  {
  do
    {
      delay(5); // Wait for switch to be released
    }
```

```
    while (digitalRead(SWITCH_PIN) == LOW);

    // Switch was released.
    delay (5); // debounce delay
    thisMode++; // Increment the program mode
    if (thisMode >= 4) // If it maxes out, reset to zero
    {
      thisMode =0;
    }
    Serial.print("Software Mode Now = "); // Say the mode
    Serial.println(thisMode,DEC);
  }

// If bit zero of thisMode is set, then the LED is on.
  if (thisMode & 1)
  {
    digitalWrite(LED_PIN,HIGH);
  }
  else
  {
    digitalWrite(LED_PIN,LOW);
  }

// If bit one of thisMode is set, then advance the motor angle.
  if (thisMode & 2)
  {
    theAngle+=3;
    if (theAngle >=150) // Are we at end of desired travel for mtr?
    {
      theAngle = 0;      // We are: reset the motor back to home pos
    }
    myMotor.write(theAngle);
  }

  delay(75);
  if (theAngle==0) // If we just reset the motor, give it time to get home.
  {
    delay(1500);
  }

}
```

As previously alluded to, you could easily extend this program to receive input via the serial channel to take commands or set the mode. Look at the software for the "WordDune" project (see Chapter 3) for an example of serial channel functions of this type.

The Moiré Wheel

Before the era of animated graphics and CGI, the moiré wheel was a beloved staple of sci-fi films and TV show set designers. This wheel creates a pretty simple but very striking effect. You print a fine mesh pattern on two transparent surfaces. You shine a bright light behind them, hold one still and slowly move the other one back and forth across the moiré pattern point. The intersection points of the lines form a morphing grid pattern. When the eye views this pattern, it resolves the result into forming and deforming shapes which come and go with a pleasing fluidity.

If you want a taste of this effect you can get it quite easily. It's only enough to give you the right idea–not as good as the finished effect, but it gives you a preview without much effort!

You'll need some thin (60 gsm or less) printer paper. Use a graphics package or the "draw" facility of your word processor to make a page containing a couple of oblong boxes on a single page. Specify no outline and set the fill pattern to be a hatched, as Figure 5-15 shows:

Figure 5-15. *An example hatched pattern that could be used on your Moire wheel*

As long as both boxes have the same lined pattern, it doesn't matter whether the lines are diagonal (as in my example), vertical, or horizontal.

Print the page containing the boxes, using the best print quality available to you. If your printer is not reproducing the lines very well, try using a fill pattern where the lines are a bit bolder and not as close together. You can still get the same effect with less dense patterns; it's just less intense.

Now, cut the page in half with scissors. Find a bright light (e.g., the LED we used in the last project, or just a regular 100W house lightbulb should do). Hold the page halves one on top of the other, right in front of the light. Hold one of the pages steady while you slowly rotate the other one. As long as enough light is getting through the paper (you'll need thinner paper or brighter light if not) you should at some point see the waves formed by the changing intersections. This gives you a rough idea of what the real thing will look like! So much for the art side of the project! Now, how do we make it?

You'll need the following things:

- A couple of transparent discs, made of fairly rigid plastic. I'd suggest using discs of between 3" and 5" (76-127 mm) across, but the size and type of these are up to you. They must be the same size and must be transparent (or almost transparent) plastic. A few possible sources:

  - Raid the recycling. Quite a lot of consumer goods and foods are packed in semirigid transparent plastic boxes or trays. You may find something you can cut discs from in that line.

  - Your local artist's shop will sell various thicknesses of clear plastic. Go for a thickness that's not floppy, but which is still transparent and easily cut to shape with normal household scissors.

  - DVD or CD recordable "cake box" packs. Most of these come with a "guard disc" at top or bottom (sometimes both) of the disc stack. These are DVD-sized discs, but they are uncoated and therefore almost transparent. You may already have some of these around, but if not, think of someone you know who burns a lot of discs (perhaps at work) and see if he or she would save some guard discs for you. They almost certainly throw them out in large numbers anyway.

  - Your local Home Depot, DIY store, or garden center may have some clear plastic sheet that you could use. These kinds of materials are often used for greenhouses, or secondary glazing for outhouse windows.

▒ **Note** Don't forget, your disc will need to have a center hole. If it doesn't already have one, you'll need to make a center hole of at least 1/4" (about 6 mm) to allow the center spindle through.

- Some spray-on acrylic varnish. This goes by various names and is used to seal a surface, much like a brush applies varnish. Own-brand products tend to be a cheaper than branded ones and work just as well. You need a spray can; brush-on products won't work in this application. I used a product called triple thick by Krylon.

- Some inkjet (or laser) decal waterslide paper. This is sold under various names and brands. Most office supply outlets will have it, and you can buy it online from Amazon and eBay among many others. Just search for "waterslide decal inkjet" and you'll find lots of vendors. We'll look at how to use this stuff in just a while.

- A +5V servo motor–just like the one we used earlier for the shadow puppets.

- A long thin bolt that can screw into the center hole on the motor shaft. It needs to be a couple of inches long ideally. This bolt is needed to couple the drive shaft of the motor to the uppermost of your plastic discs. You will also need some way to secure your plastic disc to the center bolt. In my prototype I used two of the supplied horns that came with the servo motor. Using a nut, I was able to secure the disc to the center bolt (see Figure 5-19).

Figure 5-16 shows the general arrangement.

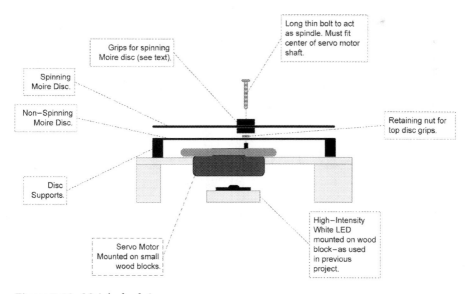

Figure 5-16. *Moiré wheel rig*

Waterslide Decals

If you have already used waterslide decals in the past and you're comfortable with using then, please feel free to skip this section. Waterslide paper lets you print transparent designs (photos, logos, moiré patterns, or whatever you want) onto a film that you can detach from its backing and affix to any plastic, metal, or glass surface. You can use it for decorating surfaces such as windows, plastic lunchboxes, or whatever else you might want.

My favorite use for waterslide paper is making light boxes. If you put a waterslide photo on a piece of thin white Plexiglas or Lexan and backlight it with a white or colored LED string you can get a lovely effect–a smaller version of the light boxes you see in stores and that light up advertising displays (see photo in Figure 5-17). If you have the skills, you could make a grid of these backlit boxes and have your own backlit photo gallery! You could use an AVR board and ULN2803 chip combination (see waterfall lights project in Chapter 4) to fade these up at down at will.

Figure 5-17. *Example of using waterslide on a backlit light box*

Sadly, I have found that it's only possible to use waterslide film with comparatively small photos (maximum 5" square is my recommendation) because it can crease and tear at larger sizes. I did once do an 8" × 10" but it was far from perfect and took several tries.

Another use I have found is making low-cost 5" touch panels. This method is limited in scope but quite a lot cheaper than using a LCD screen. In my version, the "press buttons" are on a backlit slide (similar to the one in Figure 5-17) and you overlay the image with a cheap four- or five-wire touch screen. Your software then uses touch coordinates to figure out which of the graphical buttons is being tapped. Of course, this approach is only good for applications where one set of permanent buttons is needed. It's no good for multilevel menu systems. Also, if you want to vary the button layout, you have to remake the backlit image. However, if used in appropriate situations, it makes a vivid and good-looking touch panel, at quite low cost as compared to the LCD approach.

So, how do we use this stuff? Waterslide paper arrives as what looks like standard sheets of photo paper. However, if you look closely you will see that it's actually a piece of paper with a film bonded to one side of it. The idea is that you print your design onto the film (shiny) side of it, using your normal printer (in color or monochrome). I usually try to do two or three designs at once. The waterslide paper is not cheap and so it makes sense to batch up your usages of it. You'll also find that you will spoil some of your designs and have to try again, especially at first.

Having printed your designs, you then roughly cut up the paper into pieces, each of which will contain a design you want to transfer.

Next, comes a very important step: spray at least three (preferably four or five) thin coats of acrylic varnish on. This coat seals the printed surface to protect it against moisture (as you know, inkjet print is easily washed away by moisture). Allow each coat to dry (it takes about 20–30 minutes) before applying the next. Make sure you keep count of how many coats you have put on.

▓ **Caution**   Many of these kinds of products give off nasty fumes; be sure to work in a *well-ventilated* area! Open a window or turn on an extractor fan if there is one.

You'll need a "wet area" such as a sink or drainer to do the next bit. When the last coat of acrylic varnish is dry, prepare a bowl of clean water and get your target surface (in the moiré wheel project, it will be your plastic discs) close to the water bowl ready to have the film applied to them. It can help to dampen the target surface with clean water beforehand.

Place the waterslide paper into the bowl of water (cover it with water). It will immediately try to roll up around itself. Try to prevent it from rolling up, or if it rolls up before you can stop it, gently unroll it back to a flat shape, while it's still in the water. After you have done this, it should be happy to stay reasonably flat. If the ink is starting to come off the paper at this stage then, you didn't apply enough coats of acrylic varnish and you'll probably have to start over! After 30-50 seconds it should become easy to slide the film off the backing paper. Slowly and carefully lift it away from the backing paper. As quickly as you can, transfer the film onto the target surface. If you dampened the target surface you should, at first, be able to slide the film into position (thus the name) but only for a very short time. Apply the film to the target surface as smoothly as you can. Start from the center and using a smooth cloth or a plastic sponge in a wiping motion, gently smooth out any air bubbles that get trapped or creases that may form. It's pretty easy to tear the film at this stage, so be gentle. Be prepared to mess up and have to start again a few times before you get the knack.

When you have the film applied successfully, leave it to dry for an hour or two. Then, trim off any excess film from the edges of the target surface. Hey, presto! You have a light-transparent surface with your own design on it. Yes, you *can* use this technique for full sheets of waterslide paper, but don't expect it to be easy: this technique is most useful when the designs concerned are no more than about half a normal printed page.

Building the Moiré Wheel Project

By now you should have applied your moiré patterns to both discs using the techniques described in the previous section and trimmed off the excess (don't forget to open up the center hole of the disc). The next step is to secure the top disc to the spindle (see Figure 5-16). I used a 0.1" (M2.5) bolt that was about 1" (25 mm) long. This bolt screws very nicely into the center of the servo motor.

I found that I could use two of the horns (one on top of the disc and one underneath it) that came with the servo motor along with a retaining nut underneath, to grip the disc firmly and secure it to the spindle (see Figures 5-18 through 5-20). However, you will have to take a view of what suits your needs when you have the materials and parts at hand. Some large metal washers with small center holes would do the job too.

The bottom disc does not move; it simply needs to be held to position at the required height. If, like me, you're only building a temporary version of this project, you just need to hold it steady at roughly the right height. I found some metal spacers that were approximately the right height. If you can't find anything suitable you could try using something like blocks of blu-tack. You need to position the fixed (lower) disc so that it is close to, but not touching, the moving (upper) disc. If the discs are too far apart, the moiré effect will be lessened. The fixed disc needs to allow the spindle to rotate freely, but the disc must not touch the spindle, so its center hole should be quite a lot larger than the spindle.

The underlight can be provided either by a LED string or by the high-intensity LED that we used in the shadow puppet project.

Finally, Figures 5-18 through 5-20 show the prototype rig.

This first photo show a close-up of one of the uncoated CD discs I used. This view of the disc is after the waterslide film carrying the mesh pattern has been applied to it but before trimming.

Figure 5-18. *Close-up of uncoated disc*

Figure 5-19. *Side View of the Moire Wheel Rig*

This is a side view of the entire rig. You can see the upper disc is held onto the spindle by the horns borrowed from the servo motor kit.

If I were building a permanent version of this project I think I would try to build it into a cylindrical enclosure with a reflector at the bottom in order to minimize light loss and make sure that the wheels get maximum light through them.

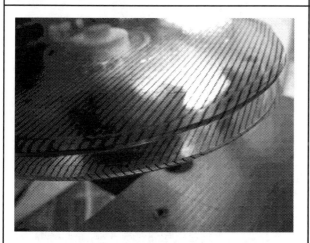

Figure 5-20. *A view of the discs*

A closer view of the two discs with the light shining through them from underneath.

Looking through the two discs with the mesh patterns at the start of the moiré zone.

Figure 5-21. Looking through the two discs

The circuit diagram we need for this project is exactly the same as we used for the shadow puppet project in Figure 5-14. The software is different.

Moiré Wheel Software

The software for this project only has to do one thing–slowly and smoothly move the servo motor back and forth in the "moiré zone." Once you have built up the project you will see that you get the most pleasing effects (the moiré zone) within a comparatively small area of movement. You'll need to find this zone by experiment since it will depend on what line pattern you used and the relative mounting positions of your discs. You can, if you prefer, just let the servo motor sweep up and down its full arc of travel (the software starts from this assumption) and you will be sure to see a moiré effect at some point during each sweep.

If you do want to tune into the moiré zone, you'll need to hook up the project's TTL serial channel to your desktop. As you will recall, the Arduino servo motor library abstracts the angle of the motor for us. So all we have to do is set start and end values in the software. This allows us to quite precisely control the sweep of the turning moiré wheel.

The moiré wheel software reacts to the following commands received at the serial channel:

- S–Increase the motor's sweep start point.

- s–Decrease the motor's sweep start point.

- E–Increase the motor's sweep end point.

- e–Decrease the motor's sweep end point.

- L–Toggle the state of the LED (on/off).

- M–toggle the state of the motor (stop/start)

- A–show the current state report. Shows sweep start and end points, current angle (useful when you are trying to judge moiré zone boundaries), and LED and motor on/off states.

The adjustment commands enforce bounds checking to make sure the start and end points don't collide and that the start point doesn't go below zero or the end point above MAX_ANGLE. If you were building a permanent version of this project, a worthwhile addition to the code would be to write the moiré zone values into EEPROM so that they are not lost at power off and can be remembered for the next session.

Generally I found that fairly short (50 ms) delays between motor steps give the best results. I also tried it with a more general light source, an LED string. It made the moiré effect appear over a slightly larger area but didn't really enhance it. I found that the moiré zone on my prototype was within a range of about 25 degrees of travel. Obviously that is highly specific and will vary according to the line density you use for your patterns, the spacing of the discs, and so on, but it gives you a guide at least.

The software is quite simple but rather too large to reproduce here. You can download it from the book's web site (www.apress.com/9781430244462). Following is a summary code walk:

Function Name	Commentary
Declarations	The declarations section consists of numerous #define directives to define constants for the program. These constants include the version number and assigning numbers to the pins that control the motor and the LED. The Boolean values for the LED and Motor state as well as the variable that holds the current angle of the motor position and several other variables are also declared.
setup()	In the setup() function the various I/O pins are assigned and initialized and the serial channel begun. The motor is set to its home position at 0 degrees rotation, and the program version string is printed to the serial channel.
loop()	In the main loop, the variable that contains the motor angle is incremented or decremented according to whether the motor is traveling clockwise or anticlockwise. • The program does checks to make sure that the start position is never set to be the same or more than the end position and that the current angle is never more that the absolute maximum angle of which the motor is capable (MAX_ANGLE) or less than zero, which in the context of a servo motor, makes no sense. If the user has set the end points to be different to the absolute end points then these set the points at which the direction of travel will reverse. • If one or other end of travel (either user set soft end points or absolute values) has been reached, then direction reverses.

(continued)

135

Function Name	Commentary
	Having calculated the new angle, the program writes it out to the PWM pin controlling the servo motor. Finally the loop() calls the serialInput() function.
serialInput()	This function checks for input from the user via the TTL level serial channel. If anything has been received, it is fetched and parsed and actioned accordingly. Unrecognized inputs are discarded and ignored.
report()	This function outputs the current state of the application's variables. It shows the state of the LED, the motor (on or off), the current angle of the motor, and the current user set start and end points.

Summary

In this chapter we have looked at three fairly different ways of using AVR controlled movement (actual or simulated). As discussed at the outset of the book, the ways in which you can use a microcontroller to create and control movement are effectively unlimited. None of the ideas or techniques presented in this chapter are in the least bit trailblazing or earth shattering; they are just intended as examples of the kind of things that, when used in combination with other ideas of the same type, can cumulatively add up to something special.

Coming Up Next

The final chapter: Smart Home?

■ ■ ■

CHAPTER 6

Smart Home Enablers

The future almost never turns out how we think it will. The much parodied "home of the future" concepts of yesteryear all had a central controlling computer at their core. Like a spider at the center of an electronic web, this computer called all the shots when it came to controlling the automated functions within the home. It was this behemoth that controlled every aspect of the automated serving of the dog's dinner or drawing those famous motorized curtains when night fell.

In early versions of the concept, it was a basement-filling box with numerous flashing lights and hundreds of chattering relays inside it. It did, of course, have a teletype that slowly chunkered out its proclamations to the humans that notionally controlled it. Yes, home automation was the future. No doubt about it!

In later versions of the vision, the control entity became an additional desktop machine that sat alongside the existing one (or was locked away in a closet, presumably building up the heat that caused its own demise!).

In more recent times, the whole concept has undergone a rebranding. Most people working in this field now tend to use the term "Smart Home." I think that, in part, this new term was taken up enthusiastically because for many people the older term "home automation" carried the baggage of years of failed promise. However, it's also in recognition of that fact that, since the advent of cheap microprocessors and more especially MCUs, it's now possible to place numerous points of "intelligence" around the home. A central entity *may* still exist in some versions of the concept, but its role is now much more as a coordinator and facilities provider than as a direct controller.

Is Your Home Smart?

The term "Smart Home" is an imprecise one and is thus open to much abuse. Look around the modern home, look around YOUR home, is it smart? Do you find these things?

- A kettle that turns itself off when the water inside it boils.

- A heating controller that comes on at a preset time and goes off at a preset time, which you can vary by day of the week.

- A cable or satellite TV box that you can program to automatically record the shows and movies that you like—and maybe even suggest additional shows that might appeal to you.

- A motion-triggered light for that dark stairway.

- A telephone answering device.

- An oven, washing machine, or dishwasher with a timer that you can preset to come on and go off at times you preselect.

- A doorbell device that can play any one of 20 preset tunes that you can select.

- Remotely controlled power sockets that you can activate with a small remote.

- A wireless network that allows you to hop onto the Internet on any one of a dozen different kinds of devices from anywhere in your home.

- A computer with a library of music, video, and family photos on it.

You probably do find many of these items—and other things besides. So is yours a Smart Home already? Twenty-five years ago, people would have probably said that, yes, these things did indeed add up to a Smart Home! But look again at the list above. Most of these things have embedded in them islands of intelligence or automation, but do they talk to one another? Do they make one another aware of what they are doing? Probably not. This goes to the core of why the Smart Home dream has failed to deliver its full potential. In short, it's a common or garden communication problem!

A challenge! Look around and try to buy the following example products off the shelf:

- A home heating system controller that can connect to your wireless network and be commanded from your Home Theatre PC or by you from your desk at work via the Internet.

- A music player for your car that you can fill up with music or speech content wirelessly from your home music library via Wi-Fi.

- A doorbell that "knows" there is nobody home and therefore plays randomly spaced barking dog sounds if the doorbell is rung.

Yes, all of these things can be done and, yes, for serious money you *can* even buy some of them from high-end specialist vendors! However, due to their high prices, they are just techno-toys for well-heeled tech enthusiasts. For the Smart Home concept to actually succeed on a large scale, something fundamental has to change to allow the whole thing to go commodity. That thing can be summed up in one word: standards.

Very few of the available Smart Home components can talk directly to one another, and no major manufacturers of household goods has been persuaded of the merit of building in support for one of the putative standards (for example, X.10, which is the closest thing to a predominant standard, especially in the US) for their mainstream products. With almost all household goods now having one or more MCUs at their heart, you would think that it would be pretty easy to make almost any household device talk TCP/IP in some way, but no, seems like there's no demand for it.

Well, that's demonstrably not true. The enthusiastic adoption over the last 25 years of the kind of devices listed above conclusively proves that we really *do* want intelligent devices doing things for us in our homes. But we want the kind of set-and-forget simplicity that we have become accustomed to from computers and computer networks. Thus Smart Home products would have to abandon proprietary approaches in hardware and do other things such as perhaps adopting standard object models (see Chapter 6 of *Practical AVR Microcontrollers* [Apress, 2012]). In other words, the Smart Home industry needs to backtrack and learn from the IT industry, which realized many years ago that if you make your hardware and software interoperate as seamlessly as possible, pretty much everybody wins. The idea that the connected, automated, or Smart Home is going to become commonplace while there is no universal plug and play compatibility between any intelligent device that you might care to buy is delusional.

In a very selfish sense, the fact that you can't buy cooperating Smart Home components at your local corner store is good news for the readers of this book! It means that the MCU enthusiast holds trump cards in his or her hand when it comes to Smart Home making. You have the ability to make your own smart devices and you probably have the knowledge to engineer interfaces to allow at least some of those stubbornly isolationist smart devices referred to above to interoperate with one another. This chapter explores this area in a little bit of detail. Of course, there are whole books on the subject of home automation and the Smart Home, so in just this one section of this one book we can only skim the surface by looking at a few techniques to make communication easier, but let's make a start!

Hacking is the name of the game when it comes to compensating for the lack of Smart Home equipment standards. All consumer products have a user interface of some sort; if you can find out how that user interface works, then you can use your MCU to pretend to be a real user. Let's start with a prime example: a remote controlled power socket.

Socket Cracking

It's very easy now to buy power sockets that you can switch on and off with a supplied remote control. How these look obviously varies from country to country since power outlet formats vary so much. Most DIY stores stock these products in some format and of course you can also get them from the usual electronics outlets.

- www.homedepot.com (US), search for product number 100654961 (indoor remote kit)

- www.maplin.co.uk (UK), stock code N79KA (3-pack remote control sockets)

These products send a coded signal from a handset to one or more power socket extensions to tell them to switch on or off. Usually you can buy these in single, three, or sometimes sets of five.

For your purposes, the main limitation of these things is that they only let you control the socket on/off state via the supplied remote control. There is (of course) no other interface; you can't command it from your Wi-Fi network or from the USB port of your PC or anything as useful as that!

So, how would you go about incorporating these sorts of products in your Smart Home setup? Say you wanted to be able to command one of these devices from a desktop computer via a USB port; how might you do that? There are two ways: a mainly software way and a mainly hardware way.

The software way consists of hooking up an appropriate type of electronic "ear" (sensor) to your AVR to allow it to capture the signal sent for each keypress on the remote. You then use software to record these signals into a small digital library. You can then replay the required keypress on the appropriate radio frequency when you want to simulate a keypress.[1] This approach works in much the same way as if you were recording each of the tones from a telephone keypad and then playing them back in the required order into the phone's microphone to make a phone call. There are various Arduino libraries (e.g., the Home Easy library) to help you go down this route, plus numerous online and print publication articles about how to go about capturing keypresses, etc.

You'll find that the kind of remote controls of interest in this context operate around the 315MHz or 433MHz bands depending on where in the world you are located. The remote control for your product should have a label on it showing exactly what frequency band it uses.

The software approach can be a good one. There's almost no hardware cost involved and you don't need to break open the original remote control hardware to make it work. The downside is that it won't work with some more advanced products because they use an encryption algorithm to ensure that their signals are unique each time. That means that recording what they "say" during one session won't do you any good because what they say during the next session will be different and what you have captured will be stale and not work. With these kinds of products, you must "train" senders and receivers to recognize one another right after their first power up. If the products you are using don't need any training, then you're probably okay to go the software route!

The hardware approach is actually very simple but it will invalidate your warranty on the product! Just to be clear, I'm *not* kidding; making the modification to be described here will definitely invalidate *any* warranty you may have on the product. So, work carefully and use anti-static precautions when handling the electronic parts.

All you need to do is take apart your remote control and use the contacts of a small relay that your software will pulse to make the relay contacts bridge the same contacts that the buttons on the remote control use. You'll need to use a driver to enable your MCU to drive the relay. You could use a 2803a chip (as you used in various other projects) to activate your relay. Don't forget to use the snubber diodes inside the 2803a to deal with the back-EMF. If you need to refresh your memory about the 2803a and snubber diodes, take a look at Figure 4-21 in Chapter 4 of *Practical AVR Microcontrollers* (Apress, 2012).

Often there's just one little recessed screw to allow you to disassemble the remote control. But sometimes the hardest part is getting the remote control apart! Some of these products clip-fit together; you'll find a tiny slot where you can insert a very small screwdriver to prise the top and bottom of the case apart. Other times there is a small but continuous groove all the way around the product; if you get a small flat blade screwdriver and carefully run it around the groove, pressing down fairly hard, you will release some little tabs inside it that hold the two halves of the product shell together. Careful how you do this; keep your fingers well out of the way!

---

[1]If your interest is more in the area of hacking TV-style IR remotes, have a look at Ken Shiriff's excellent Arduino IR Library at `www.arcfn.com/2009/08/multi-protocol-infrared-remote-library.html`.

Other times the manufacturers hide the fixing screw under a label. If you suspect this is how your remote control is made, get the handle end of your screwdriver and rub it firmly around the label face. Then, hold the label up to a bright light and you should be able to see the indent of the screwhole. Pierce the label at that point and you should be able to disassemble.

Once you have your remote control apart, you should easily be able to see how the buttons, when pressed, bridge the sets of contacts. It's up to you to decide how many buttons you want to extend out of the remote, but it's usually a very simple job to add wires to the contact points and bring them out to the contacts of a small relay that your MCU can control. The resulting solution may not be especially elegant, but it will allow your MCU to easily control main devices in a very safe way. Usually you can hide away the wired-up remote control.

On the Radio: The Un-wired Home

As stated earlier, we can't address the massive subject of the Smart Home in a few pages of one book, but one area that seems worth spending some pages exploring—and looking at just one pragmatic solution—is the crucial area of communications.

One particular barrier to Smart Home communication is wiring. Unless you're lucky enough to be closely involved with planning, building, or completely gutting and renovating your home, running a cable to the location of each and every little device that you may want to participate in your Smart Home is quite an undertaking!

Just thinking about the AVR level of Smart Home making: you'd need to have everything from a smart bell push for the front door to a smart door sensor, temperature sensors, motion sensors, light sensors, smart locks, entry keypads, lighting controllers... the list is a potentially very long one, even before you start adding your higher-end multimedia terminals, digital music and video streaming, and so on. Are you really going to run a CAT5 or CAT6 cable for each one of these things?

There are, of course, many alternatives to running wires to each and every little AVR powered device around your Smart Home.

- Wi-Fi—802.11b/g: This is superficially attractive because you are quite likely to have a Wi-Fi network in your home already, so what could be neater than having your Smart Home devices tap into it? Logistically true, but financially flawed. Look at price of a Wi-Fi module that works with (for example) an Arduino. You'll be doing well if you can find one for less than $40 US, and it won't even be a complete solution; you'll need to add some extra stuff to make it actually work with your AVR. Add the cost of your AVR (or an Arduino, if you go that route). Multiply that by the number you will require and... well, the numbers don't look attractive.

- There are many products available now that let you make Ethernet network connections through the mains wiring of your house; this is often called powerline networking. These products work really well in most situations (though they are not legal to use in all countries as yet, so do check the local legalities). But again, explore the cost-per node: add up the cost of a mains network interface and the Ethernet module you will need to allow your MCU to be an Ethernet end node. Multiply the cost per node by the number of Smart Home peripherals you think you might need and see if your eyes don't water! By my reckoning you're looking at about $60 per node, minimum, at the time of writing!

- Zigbee is another wireless networking standard that is much vaunted by the Smart Home movement, but again, unless product prices fall (another case of a minimum $50 per viable node at the time of writing), this is not really not going to find its way into high-volume consumer products any time soon.

- There are other alternatives such as Bluetooth, which is more viable financially, coming in at about half the price of the solutions above. However, anything using a Bluetooth solution has to go through the overhead (and delay) of pairing at start-up and handling connection drops and so on.

- There are other basic ways to do certain kinds of wireless connections and these are far lower cost. We'll take a look at one of these options in the "Low-Cost Wireless Communication" section later in this chapter.

Wiring Up

So, clearly the wireless route has the potential to be fairly high cost. However, you may think that is a price worth paying in order to save having to run (and live with) all that wiring. Returning to the subject of wiring, where exactly is the problem?

Many Smart Home setups feature a radial wiring plan. In other words, there is some central point to which each and every cable goes back (see Figure 6-1). This central point is often a wiring shelf in a closet or (in a large home) a utility room containing a wiring hub in a floor standing cabinet. The nodes of the network derive their power from the nearest mains outlet.

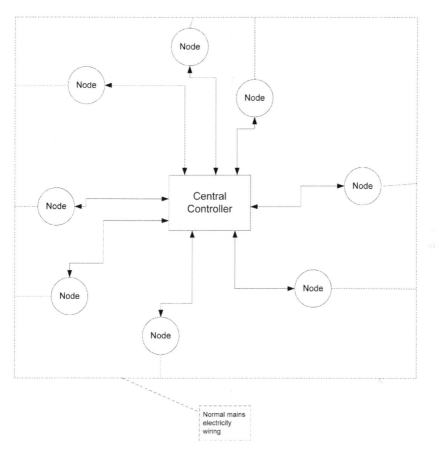

Figure 6-1. *Smart Home radial connection—central control*

Nodes can be anything from a desktop computer to a door sensor. This radial wiring approach goes back to the original notion of having a single controlling entity at a single point in the Smart Home. As outlined earlier, it goes all the way back to the days when the cost of the controlling central computer was the biggest price ticket item in the whole enterprise, back to the days when the control computer was the single most unique and complex item in the whole setup.

However, thanks in large measure to the MCU, the radial wiring approach now has competition; as described earlier in this chapter, the intelligence in a modern setup can be much more distributed. In this alternative model, there doesn't need to be a central point. There is simply a network connection linking all points in some way. It may be a simple daisy chain, as in Figure 6-2. In this model, the central controller has been simplified to a resource server. For example, it may simply issue network addresses or it may offer hard drive storage for nodes to send logging data to.

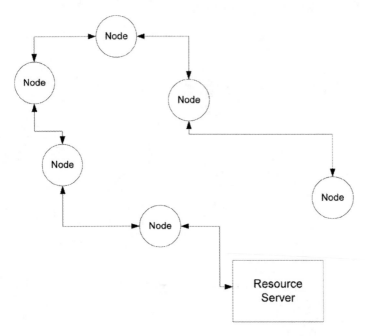

Figure 6-2. *Smart Home daisy chain wiring*

A more mixed scheme, as shown in Figure 6-3, might also be used. This is no longer a daisy chain; it is a fairly random arrangement with the only requirement being that all nodes on the network can "hear" one another in some way. In this model of operation, nodes can have the ability to generate events and to consume events and autonomously act upon them (again, see the discussion in Chapter 6 of *Practical AVR Microcontrollers* [Apress, 2012]).

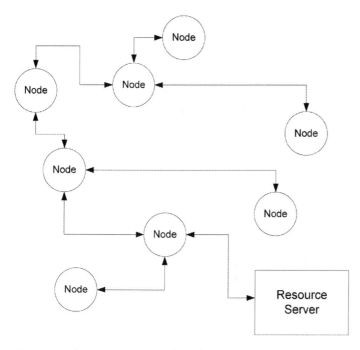

Figure 6-3. *Smart Home—mixed topology*

Back to Basics

Going back to basics, what you need is, in many cases, incredibly simple. If you referred to Chapter 6 of *Practical AVR Microcontrollers* (Apress, 2012), you saw that, with proper and tight design of your communications, messages can be very compact. For example, in the SHOM (Smart Home Object Model) imagineered there,[2] the 5-byte sequence shown in the following table conveys all the information that is required for a sensor node to communicate its state:

Byte #	Means
1	1 = Fittings
2	5 = Windows
3	1 = Sensors
4	8 = Window number 8 (rear, ground floor, kitchen)
5	2 = Event code (might mean has gone from closed state to open state)

---

[2]Please remember that SHOM is not any kind of standard; it's just something I invented to show how a slim protocol can be developed for use within a closed environment.

For conveying something so small, some of the connection methods listed above (and their associated costs) somehow seem like using the proverbial sledgehammer to crack a nut! Of course, as you saw in "Digitally Speaking" you'd have to add some kind of jacket around the basic 5-byte packet plus a header and some checksum protection. Even so, the whole message in this example would be unlikely to be more than 15 bytes long.

In fact, in a network like the one in Figure 6-3, many of the nodes will be very trivial ones, such as a window sensor, a light level detector, a doorbell button, a phone ring detector, etc. These kinds of nodes are very easily implemented using a very cheap, low-end AVR; it doesn't have to offer a lot of I/O lines and it doesn't need a lot of memory. Each one only needs to do the following things:

- Interface with a sensing or switching element (for example, the window open sensor).

- Have the ability to be programmed with an ID. Going back to the SHOM example, it needs to know that it is a node of type Fittings\ Windows\Sensor, it is sensing the open/closed state of window number 8, and the event code to generate for any given sequence of sensor inputs.

- It needs to be given some kind of interface to allow it to participate in the local network.

All except the last item on this list can easily be met by using a low-end 8-pin AVR costing just a couple of dollars, but what about that last item?

Low-Cost Wireless Communication

If you want to embrace the idea of having a Smart Home in which you can embed intelligence everywhere at an affordable price, you need to think pragmatically. There are low-cost wireless products that you can use; they can be bought (from Asian vendors) for as little as $5 for a transmitter module *and* a receiver module. These are usually sold as "xxMHz receiver transmitter modules" by various electronics sites (where xx is usually 433 in much of Europe and 315 or 434 in North America).

- www.sparkfun.com/products/10534 (US) Transmitter

- www.sparkfun.com/products/10532 (US) Receiver

- www.techsupplies.co.uk (UK) (search for RFA001 and related items)

Many companies seem to make these. Two typical ones that I have used are shown in Figure 6-4. The transmitter module is on the right and it has the following three pins:

- +Vcc (typically between 4.5 and 9 Volts)

- Ground

- TXdata (a logic-compatible input)

Figure 6-4. *Low-cost short range radio modules*

The receiver is on the left and it has four pins, though only three are actually used. These carry

- +Vcc

- Ground

- RXdata (a logic-compatible output)

Both modules easily plug into a breadboard (though you may need to add some header pins).

Make sure that the modules you buy have logic level (TTL/CMOS) compatible inputs and outputs and can operate on +5Volts. Most such products seem to meet these requirements, but do check before buying. The modules require the addition of an antenna (see bullet point, below).

The essential idea is that you connect the serial port pins (transmit and receive) of the AVR to the radio modules and, using a port speed of 2400 baud (as opposed to the more usual 9600), you can exchange data across the resulting link. There are some important things to be aware of when using these modules:

- The modules MUST use a wavelength (e.g., 433MHz) that is license exempt in your geography. Your vendor can advise. *Do not* import modules from another country and assume they will be okay; license-exempt frequencies vary from place to place.

- The communication they provide is usable over only very short distances inside a home. About 20 feet (approx. 6 meters) seems to be an optimum (see below) using just a wire antenna. If you are willing to use a more elaborate antenna, you will get a far greater range but at more cost and trouble.

- They are in no sense intelligent. They do no packetization of the data to be sent; neither do they offer guaranteed delivery of that data or *any* error checking.

- They are not secure. Anyone sitting outside your home with sufficiently sensitive listening equipment could listen in to the traffic passing between these modules.

Looking at the kinds of applications you have in mind, the second and third items on this list are not necessarily big problems. If you can install a small number of wired hubs around the home (hidden in ceiling voids, crawl spaces, closets, etc.), those can act as signal relays. Then you only require short distance transmission to the nearest hub node. Because they only communicate occasionally, many wireless nodes can talk to a single hub. As for these being very dumb devices, you're using an AVR in each end node and the intelligence can be built into the software of that.

As for the final item on the list, it's true that anybody with a malicious intent and the right knowledge could start commanding your Smart Home to do some wacky stuff! So you do need to be aware of this when deciding when to use this approach and when to use more expensive ones. You'll look at this in more detail in a short while.

Security is always an issue, and sadly, most wireless security protocols seem to get cracked (a quick Google search can verify this), so you should never assume that you can attain total security in wireless communications of any kind. Later in this chapter you'll look at some more detailed cases for deciding whether to use low-cost wireless or not.

Smart Home Using a Mixed Network

What would a Smart Home network built using a mix of short range radio modules and wired hubs look like? It might look something like the diagram in Figure 6-5, in which you might still have your resource server (though it's not mandatory) and a handful of wired hub nodes. Each wired node acts as a highly localized area hub, located near a cluster of wireless nodes. If the diagram brings to your mind a picture of many desktop-grade machines scattered around the home, jammed into closets, hidden under beds, or perched precariously on top of bookshelves, forget it! It's more likely that

- The hub nodes would be something like an Arduino in a box, equipped with an Ethernet CAT6 (or perhaps the compatible, but older CAT5) interface and with a low-cost radio transmitter and receiver attached to its serial port. Alternatively, it might be a naked AVR (see Chapter 3 of *Practical AVR Microcontrollers* [Apress, 2012]!) board of your own devising.

- The wireless nodes would be controlled by a very low-end AVR chip with a low cost radio module attached, built into something no larger than the size of a couple of matchboxes. Possibly it would be battery powered or it might just need to plug into a USB power adaptor to any nearby mains power socket.

- The resource server could be an old desktop machine or laptop.

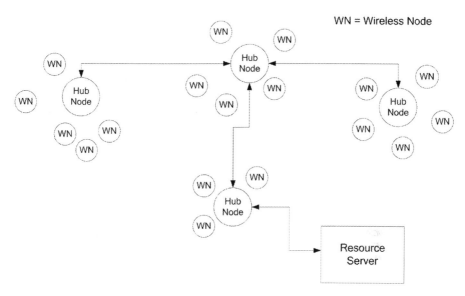

Figure 6-5. *Mixed network, wired and wireless*

The wired network might be a completely separate one from the one you use for your desktop machines, or it might be the same one. If it were separate, the resource server could be set to route traffic between the two LANs.

The possibility (make that, probability!) that some of the data that these kinds of nodes send will be lost, or could be heard by a third party, is a deciding factor in whether you use a wireless or wired node.[3]

The following are some examples of where datapath reliability or security is important and where it is not:

- Case 1: A movement sensor that is intended to trigger some lights might be connected over a short-distance radio link. If a person enters the room, the sensor is triggered and the node to which the sensor is attached broadcasts a message on the network, indicating that this movement trigger has been activated. Another node that is monitoring for such event notifications is supposed to turn the light on, but it never "sees" the movement sensor event because the network is busy. The person who triggered the light and has gotten used to the lights turning on when she enters the room simply does what we all do in such circumstances, she waves her arms around. This time the system works and the lights come on; no big deal, just so long as it doesn't happen every time.

---

[3]In passing, it's worth noting that even unencrypted traffic on a wired LAN *can* be listened to outside of your home by someone with sufficiently sensitive equipment—though such equipment is said to be very expensive.

- Case 2: A flame sensor is connected over a short-distance wireless link. The flame sensor senses a flame: a log has spilled out of the open fire and onto a carpet. The node to which the sensor is connected sends out a message that is supposed to raise the alarm, but the data packet it sends never makes it. A sprinkler system controller is listening for flame sensor triggers but never sees the alarm. Bad news!

- Case 3: A door entry system that allows a code to be entered on a keypad and then sends the entered code to a superior system via radio; it receives back an "Open" or "Don't Open" response.

So, in the first case, you don't really care if data is lost because the consequences are pretty trivial—just a minor temporary annoyance. However, in the second case, you do care a *lot* and that node should never have been made wireless! Case 3 should never be wireless because a listener could easily intercept the keycode they need to be able to get through the door.

In summary, if it's just a matter of somebody knowing when your door opens or closes, do you care? If they start commanding your feature lights to go on and off, well, it's pretty easy to disable that feature until they get tired of the game. However, for other things, this low-cost approach is not sensible to use and you will have to use a more expensive setup. Yes, this kind of wireless connection has limitations, but it is a very useful and low-cost way to avoiding running wires around your home for a significant number of purposes, especially for simple sensors or lighting control.

Taking the earlier project of the waterfall lights (the passageway lighting system) as an example, if you added a wireless sender module to that, it could send out a log of its activations and status. If you added a send-and-receive module, it could receive commands to switch on and receive updates, for example to the length of time it stayed on, based on an analysis of sensor log data collected over a period of time. If you had a house security controller, the waterfall light could receive "nobody home mode" messages that would make it ignore any sensor activations that might be made by the dog or cat wandering around.

In short, if the less critical elements of a Smart Home setup could be implemented with a cheap and easy way to allow it to contribute information into a Smart Home network, then many things would change! This approach is very much in line with initiatives like VSCP (Very Simple Control Protocol), which aim to allow cheap and simple Smart Home implementations by simplifying and commoditizing the design and topology involved.

A Simple HomeHelp Protocol

As outlined in the previous section, the low-cost radio modules do not have any embedded intelligence—none at all! They simply act as a data pipe, a radio version of a cable, except not so reliable! As you saw, data can fail to make it from one end of the pipe to the other or can be garbled en-route.

In order to be sure that you receive correct data, you need to invent a protocol that performs a number of functions:

- It allows the receiving node to distinguish between random radio noise and actual data.

- It provides a description of the data being sent.

- It provides a mechanism to provide a reasonable amount of assurance that the data that has been received is the same as the data that was sent.

- It identifies the sender and intended recipient so that, in your mixed network where all the nodes can "hear" what each another are saying, they can tell whether a data packet is something they need to pick up and look at or not.

- It provides an extensible packet scheme that can be upgraded in future while still retaining backwards compatibility if that should prove to be necessary, so that network nodes which have not been upgraded can still operate using the previous version of the protocol.

The protocol to be presented here is a simple one, but one that provides all of the functions that were listed above. It is a connectionless protocol, which means it only allows single messages to be passed from one radio equipped node to another one. There is no concept of a reply to a message and no handshaking, which means that nothing in the protocol allows the sender to know if the receiver has got the sent message or not. In networking terms, this is "best endeavor" communication—no guaranteed delivery and no failure notifications.

The HomeHelp protocol, version 1, packet layout is shown in the following table (all values in decimal unless otherwise noted):

Area Name	Byte Number	Type	Binary Values	Details
HomeHelp Packet Header	1-6	Bytes	5-4-3-2-1-0	A simple binary countdown forming a lead-in to the packet. Seeing this sequence allows a receiver to know that a packet is coming, since it is highly unlikely to occur randomly in a noise pattern.
	7	Byte	1 to 255	A byte value indicating the version number of the packet that follows. This will, at the moment, contain the value 1, since there is only one version of this protocol. If there is ever a second issue of the protocol, this byte would allow a receiving node to know which version spec to use in processing the rest of the packet.
	8-9	Unsigned int (16 bits)	0-65535	"To Node:" A 16-bit unsigned integer indicating to which local node this packet is addressed. This is sent low byte first. Special values:
				0 = Broadcast, all nodes should take notice
				1 to 31 (0x1F) = Reserve values, do not use
				31-65535 = Can be used as node numbers

(continued)

Area Name	Byte Number	Type	Binary Values	Details
HomeHelp Packet Header	10-11	Unsigned int (16 bits)	0-65535	"From Node:" A 16-bit unsigned integer indicating to which local node sent this packet. This is sent low byte first. Special values:
				0 = Sender is a master node
				1 to 31 (0x1F) = Reserve values, do not use
				31-65535 = Normal node numbers
	12-13	Unsigned int (16 bits)	0-65535	Payload packet size (PPS): This is a 16-bit value indicating how many bytes are in the payload that comes next. Low byte is sent first.
Payload	14-n	Bytes	--	The payload itself. This can be whatever you want, just a byte stream of n-14 bytes.
Checksum	n+1	Unsigned int (16 bits)	0-65535	This is a checksum of the payload. It uses the checksum computation scheme outlined in Chapter 6 of *Practical AVR Microcontrollers* (Apress, 2012) in which each byte in the payload is added together to make a 16-bit checksum, but the result is limited to 16 bits by discarding any arithmetic carry. This value is sent low byte first.

Obviously, in this scheme, you can put whatever you like in the payload section.

An important function of the software implementing the receiver end of this protocol is a timeout. If the channel starts delivering a packet but loses connection halfway through, it's important that the receiving software knows when to give up and abort reception; otherwise it would be stuck waiting for the rest of the packet forever and the software would stall.

Using a Low-Cost Smart Home Wireless Node

In this project, you are going to build a simple door sensor. It will send a HomeHelp format wireless data packet whenever the door state changes. This will be sent to a simple receiving module, which will then display the status in a terminal window. Since the main point here is to show how to use the short-range wireless modules, the receiver is not going to be a hub node and the payload will be a single byte, not a fully qualified SHOM sequence.

In a real implementation, you would most likely want to use an 8-pin AVR (such as maybe an ATtiny85 chip) for the door sensor project, but you've been using the ATmega328 through this book, so let's stick with that. You could, of course, rig up many sensors to this one controller, but you'll use only one sensor in this example project.

Figure 6-6 shows a block diagram of the project. In summary,

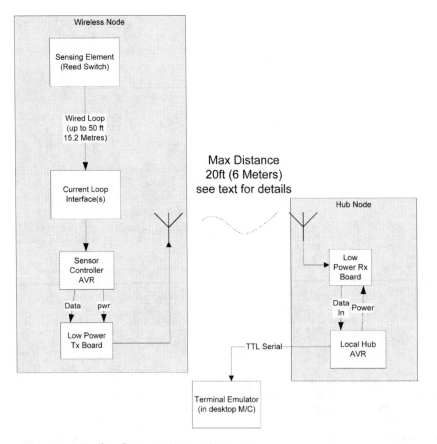

Figure 6-6. *Wireless door opening monitor*

- A door sensor is connected via a current loop isolator to a sensor controller AVR. The current loop interface allows you to have as long a cable run as you need to the door sensor; however, if you are able to locate the circuitry within a short distance from the sensor, you may be able to dispense with the current loop interface and just wire the sensor direct to an AVR input pin, thus saving the cost of the opto-coupler chip.

- The software constantly polls the state of the sensor. When a change of state is detected, it formulates an appropriate message and sends it out via the low power transmitter. Although the message is jacketed inside a HomeHelp format packet, the core of this message is very simple; it's just a single byte that takes one of the following values:

  - 01 = Started up (message sent after power on).

  - 02 = Going away (sent if controller is commanded to power off or reboot).

  - 03 = The door was closed and is now open.

  - 04 = The door was open and is now closed.

  - 05 = The door is open (sent periodically to confirm a door left open).

- The low power transmitter used in this circuit actually requires so little power that it can be powered from an AVR output pin! This allows the transmitter to be powered off by the MCU between transmissions. This reduced power supply requirement (if you used a low-power MCU such as an ATmega328-up) might make the project a candidate for battery operation, which for this kind of usage might be very handy!

- The message travels across the air to the receiver (RX) board. I have played around with several different products and ways of doing the antenna for them. I would say that, using just a wire antenna inside a home, you should regard 20 feet (about 6 meters) as the maximum distance over which you will get reasonably reliable transfer. Obviously, using more expensive sorts of antenna (and perhaps even with different makes of board) will get you different results.

- When the local hub AVR has received the message from the sensor node, it examines the contents. If the received message is valid, it decodes the meaning and puts out a message via its TTL serial channel to a terminal window running on a desktop machine.

Using just a piece of wire as the antenna, I have had communication between sender and receiver at a distance of about 40 indoor feet, but it's very variable; some days it didn't work at all. Over a distance of 20 feet, reliability is (with the setups I have tried) very good, and actually 20 feet is quite a long distance inside a home; in an average sized home it would get you from one room into the next. Usually, you would locate your hub receivers at strategic places out of sight. Such locations might include

- Up above the ceiling or in an attic space.

- In in-between floors space.

- In a crawl space.

- In a closet or under shelving.

- Under or behind a chair or couch.

- Hidden inside some piece of household equipment such as a clock.

As long as there is no radio block (such as a steel door or masonry containing lots of flint) between transmitter and receiver, you should not have a problem. You can get a lot more range albeit (at a cost that may work out to be several times more than the cost of the module!) by using a custom made antenna; however, I used a length of breadboard jumper wire, which did the job at almost zero cost.

I found that the length of the wire makes a big difference to the performance of the link. There seems to be an optimum length, so a little experimentation with different antenna wire lengths is worth the time it takes. I found that a wire between 7–9 inches (about 180mm–230mm) worked best, but I'm sure it's highly product- and situation-specific.

Door Sensor Circuit Diagram

The circuit diagram in Figure 6-7 shows the circuit diagram for the wireless sender. You could build this as a temporary breadboard project or as a separate small solder board inside a box if you want it as a permanent facility.

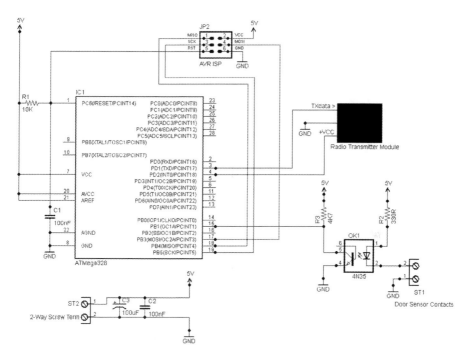

Figure 6-7. *Door sensor wireless node circuit diagram*

The MCU used is an ATmega328 (as noted earlier, you might want to use a smaller and cheaper AVR, such as an 8-pin ATmega85 in a real deployment). In this implementation,

- Pin 4 (Arduino digital in 2) is used to supply power to the radio transmitter module when needed (and only then).

- Pin 3 (Arduino TX) supplies the serial data stream to be sent over the radio transmitter module.

- Pin 15 (Arduino digital pin 9) is configured as an input to sense the state of the door switch. In the configuration shown, if the door switch is closed (i.e., the magnet is close to the sensor), then the pin will read as LOW.

- Other pins are used in the normal way for ISP programming.

The door sensor is interfaced to the MCU via an opto-coupler, which you are using as the current loop interface (see Chapter 4 of *Practical AVR Microcontrollers* [Apress, 2012], Figure 4-37, for more details). R3 is strictly redundant as you could use the internal pull-up resistor in the MCU, but you can use both if you so desire.

The power supply requirement for this project is +5Volts at a peak of 200ma; the average consumption on my prototype is only about 28ma.

Door Sensor Sender Software

The software for the door sensor project is pretty straightforward. Let's do the code walk:

Function Name and Args	Commentary
Global section	Declares all the constants, such as making the baud rate 2400, which pins to use, and the meanings of the single byte payload that the software will send.
setup() args: none	Initializes the serial channel and sets the required pin modes. Then uses sendPkt() sent out a packet with the "Started" value in it to let the receiver know it is alive.
loop() args: none	The loop function reads the door sensor state. If it's active (door open), it uses sendPkt() to send a notification. Then it waits for the door sensor to return to the inactive state; when it does, it uses sendPkt() to send out a notification of that event. It would be nice to have the function send out a packet every now and again if the door remains open for too long, since under the right circumstances it might be useful for some function higher up the pecking order (such as a security application) to know that the door remains open. Recognizing that the door has been open for longer than it should be could also be implemented higher up the chain, but that would make it possible for false alarms to be generated if the doorOpen event packet made it through, but the subsequent doorClosed packet did not.
	The function also contains various delays to allow for switch debounce times. However, these are probably not required since the packet send delays probably amount to a long enough time between detecting the first switch closure and contact bouncing ending.
	Finally, the main loop pauses for half a second before starting again.
sendPkt() args: byte payloadByte	The sendPkt() function sends a HomeHelp format packet out with the door event code as the payload. The code to be sent is supplied by the function's caller. Note that the sendPkt() function switches the radio transmitter on before it starts to send and off when it has completed. In both cases, it waits a short while to allow the transmitter to stabilize (at power up) and to complete sending (at power down).
	Since you're only, in this instance, sending a single byte value over the link, the only byte that is used to calculate the checksum is that value! Therefore, the payload byte and the checksum are, in this unique case, always the same!

Door Sensor Receiver Software

The door sensor receiver is essentially (in the terms of the mixed network topology that was previously discussed) pretending to be a hub. All it really does is receive the packet from the door sensor sender, make sure the HomeHelp jacket looks okay, and call out the value of the payload as a string to a software serial port, as in these examples:

```
Received "Started up" from node 51
Received "Door was closed, is now open" from node 51
Received "Door was open, is now closed" from node 51
```

The receiver has to use a software serial port since the hardware port is used for the radio channel.

Door Sensor Summary

The door sensor sender is a simple project, mainly intended to show how to use low-cost radio modules to bring down the cost of your Smart Home installation. Using this approach allows you to install sensors and nodes wherever you like without having the mess and hassle of installing and trying to conceal long wiring runs.

The project is an example of a node that only outputs sensor data, but what about the reverse case? What about a node that only receives data?

Remotely Commandable Light Stand

The door sensor is an example of Smart Home device that only sends data into the Smart Home network. In this, the final example Smart Home project, you will look at a receive-only example.

This project is essentially a demonstration of using Smart Home techniques to command this class of device; only a very small part of its full potential is exploited here. I'm sure that readers will see endless additional possibilities!

We're quite used to having remote control over things. We have remote control of our TVs, car alarm, DVD player, and so on. In this sample Smart Home project, you're going to give yourself remote control of a special light project: a light stand or shelf!

It turns out that if you shine light through the edge of a thick piece of transparent acrylic plastic, most of the light will, if the edges have been smoothed and polished properly, travel through the material and come out of the edges opposite. This gives a really gorgeous effect, lighting up a shelf or a stand for something special. If the light used is a multi-color LED strip, then, by varying the intensity of each LED (using PWM) you can create light in any color you want, including white when all LEDs are at equal intensity. So, in this project, you can use the short-distance radio link (as detailed in the previous project) to remotely command the Smart Home node that controls the LED strip.

Let's start with some basics: an RGB LED strip. Example products include

- www.sparkfun.com/products/10261 (United States and elsewhere)
- www.maplin.co.uk (UK; search for N48JX)

These are essentially flexible PCBs with tri-color, surface-mount LED devices fixed at regular intervals along their length. Each device actually contains three LEDS: red, green, and blue. The PCB provides a separate bus connection for the negative connections of all the reds, all the greens, and all the blue connections; there is also a +V lead that connects to all LED devices. The examples listed above use +12Volts, but I believe there may also be +5V products around if you look for them.

The strips have "cut points" marked along their length (see Figure 6-8), which present solder pads for attaching your connections (as shown in Figure 6-9).

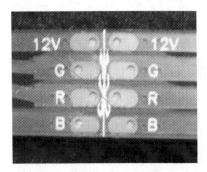

Figure 6-8. *LED strip showing cut point*

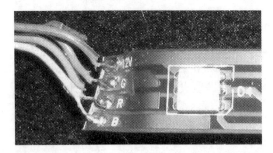

Figure 6-9. *LED strip cut and wires soldered on*

Your first decision is to decide how many lengths you want to use. I used three, which, since there are three LEDs per length, gave me nine tri-color LEDs in my setup. You could use more or less; the current consumption of the LEDs in these types of product is not huge (check your product details for specifics) so using more is fine. Having decided how many LED lengths you want to use, you should now be able to decide the sizing for your slab of plastic!

I bought my plastic shelf from an EBay vendor (there are many) who also offers a cutting and polishing service. It is made of 10mm (about 0.4″) thick transparent plastic. I chose this thickness to match the width of the LED strip to make it easy to mount the LED strip along the edge of the stand. I want to use it as a stand for a miniature MP3 jukebox; you'll see how this goes together a little later. I had the vendor cut the shape I wanted and polish all the edges. This was not especially cheap (about $35) but the result was excellent, as you can see in Figure 6-10.

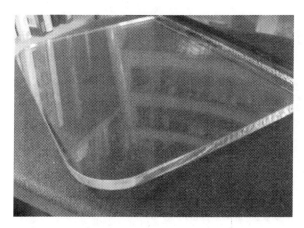

Figure 6-10. Light stand

Next, I got a plastic angle from the home improvement store (with an L-shape profile), cut it to length, and used some standard general purpose adhesive to fix it onto the plastic stand, such that it provides a channel to drop the LED strip into. The photo in Figure 6-11 shows this detail.

Figure 6-11. LED strip channel

Then, I soldered my four wires, making them about 3 feet long (2.7m) to the LED strip. Most of these LED strips come with a sticky back that allows you to stick the strip onto something. Thinking ahead, though, I imagined how hard it would be to remove this if the LED strip ever failed or if I wanted to swap it out for a different type. So, instead of using the sticky back, I put some 1" black insulating tape along the underside of the LED channel to hold the strip in place in its channel. And that was it; the light stand ready to go, as shown in Figure 6-12.

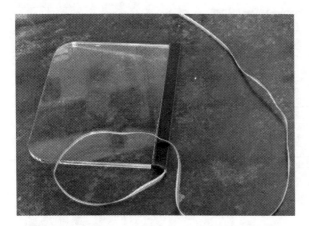

Figure 6-12. *Light stand with LED strip in place and cable attached*

Light Stand Electronics

The electronics are pretty simple. It's another two-chip project with just the ATmega328 AVR chip and a 2803 driver. However, it does requires the split rail power supply, capable of giving +12Volts for the LEDs and +5Volts for the AVR.

On the LED string product I was using, each colored LED (e.g., the red LED inside just one of the surface mounted devices) consumed a maximum of 7 milliamps. As mentioned previously, I used nine RGB devices along my LED strip. So the current requirements, in my case, were

- 9 x 7 milliamps for the red LEDs = 63 milliamps

- 9 x 7 milliamps for the green LEDs = 63 milliamps

- 9 x 7 milliamps for the blue LEDs = 63 milliamps

Thus the current requirement for the +12volt supply was, in my case, less than 200 milliamps, and the amount of current to sink for each set of colored LEDs was very easily within the capability of a 2803 chip. The full circuit diagram for the project is shown in Figure 6-13.

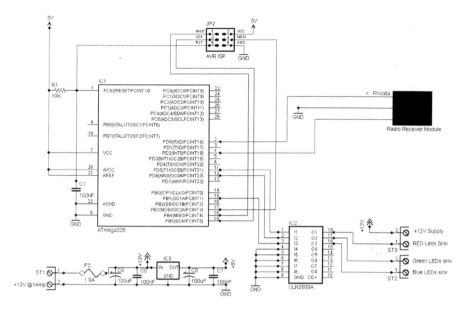

Figure 6-13. *Light stand project circuit diagram*

As you can see from the diagram, there's not an awful lot to it. The radio receiver module connects to the AVR's serial receive line. Pins 11, 12, and 15 (Arduino digital pins 5, 6, and 9, respectively) connect to the 2803A driver chip in which the first three drivers are used to sink current from the red, green, and blue LED elements, respectively. The remaining drivers in the chip are unused and their inputs grounded. The AVR's pin 4 (Arduino digital pin 2) is used to supply the minimal amount of power required by the receiver module. This allows the AVR to disable the receiver if necessary.

The RGB LED strip connects via a set of screw connectors; in a permanent version of this project you could use a small 4-way connector (see the Waterfall Lights project sensor connector for a suitable example).

Light Stand: RGB Values Sender

The software and hardware for the light stand is almost exactly the same as what you used for the door sensor. There are just three differences:

- In the hardware for this project, there is no door sensor interface.

- In the software,

  - Rather than having to wait for the door sensor to go active, the loop() function just sends a HomeHelp format packet containing a 4-byte payload consisting of a command code (which is always zero) and three randomly chosen RGB values. Such a packet is sent about every 10 seconds.

  - The checksum value is no longer a repeat of the payload; it is now properly calculated, based on the values sent in the payload.

163

The sender circuit diagram is shown in Figure 6-14.

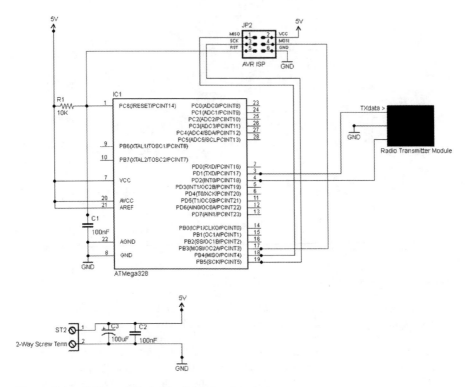

Figure 6-14. *Radio sender for the light stand project*

Aside from these differences, the hardware and software for the light stand sender are the same as those used for the door sensor sender. The payload sending order is shown in the following table:

Payload Byte #	Byte Usage
1	Command code. Currently, the only command that the receiver recognizes is zero, meaning that the remaining three bytes contain RGB values. Many more ideas are possible (see below).
2	Red value (8-bit byte): This is a PWM intensity value for the red LEDs.
3	Green value (8-bit byte): This is a PWM intensity value for the green LEDs.
4	Blue value (8-bit byte): This is a PWM intensity value for the blue LEDs.

Clearly, you could do a lot more with this. For example, you could implement anything up to 254 additional command codes for the receiver to action. Such commands might be

- Do fade up or down at some specified speed.

- Do random colors locally.

- Flash the LEDs at various speeds.

- Do a local sequence to gradually step through all possible colors over a period of n minutes.

- Do color chaser.

- Set LEDs to one of n preset colors (stored in the MCU's EEPROM).

- Do a light show.

All kinds of possibilities exist, and as always with MCUs, they are yours just for the working out!

Light Stand Software: Receiver

The software for the light stand is quite long, but in fact only consists of three functions! Let's do the code walk:

setup()	The usual setup function contents; it declares the pin numbers being used as PWM to sink the LED lines for red, green, and blue. Also declares the memory construct that holds the current values for RGB. Initializes the serial channel via which the software listens for commands coming in via the low cost short range radio. It initializes the PWM values so that the LEDs are all off. Then it declares the radio receiver pin and applies power to the receiver board.
loop()	Probably the simplest loop() function yet! It calls the getPacket() function. If the function returns a correctly received packet, the values it contained are written out to the LED PWM control pins to set the required red, green, and blue levels.
getPacket() args: timeoutMS	This function is the big one here. It receives and verifies a packet from the radio network in the format described in the "A Simple HomeHelp Protocol" section earlier in this chapter. It waits for a packet to turn up, but only for timeoutMS. If a packet is received (or begins to be received) during that window, it receives it, verifies the checksum, and if all is well, it returns success and passes back the payload in the global text buffer. If no packet is received before the timeout is reached or the packet is received in error, it returns a failure and the buffer contents will be invalid.

The code for this project is a good illustration of one of the principal things MCU chips have changed. The processor in this project will spend most of the time just whizzing around the loop() and getPacket() functions waiting for something to do! Even 20 years ago, this would be almost a crime because CPUs were a comparatively expensive resource that you had to make best possible productive use of. Back then, if you were making a project like this, you'd probably look for other things the unit could do so as not to waste any processing time.

However, MCUs (and indeed microprocessors) changed things by making processing power very, very cheap by comparison to what it had been; so now it's okay to only use a small part the available processing power productively.[4] You can have a separate processor for each little function within a system, almost the mirror image to the old-time home automation idea that you started off this chapter with (i.e., the monster computer in the basement)!

The Light Stand in Action

The photo sequence of Figure 6-15 through Figure 6-17 gives an idea of the finished result.

In this photo, the stand is illuminated in response to a radio command. The table-top jukebox lighting is off.

As you can see, the light transfer from the rear of the stand to the front is excellent. You don't get anything like as good light transmission if the edges are not highly machine polished (I tried!).

As you can probably see from the photo, the light spreads out from the front of the base in little prongs when the stand is on a flat surface (see the "from above" photo later).

Figure 6-15. Light stand on, mini-jukebox off

---

[4]Many might argue that it's bad computer science but at least now it's not compounded by being financial folly, too!

Figure 6-16. *Stand and jukebox on*

In this photo, the MP3 jukebox lights are also on, completing the effect.

If the light stand controller software was enhanced to include a set of fading and flashing effects, it would be possible to add additional items to the simple protocol to activate these via the radio command channel. This is left as a project for the reader!

The project makes an ideal addition to the décor in a themed room such as a TV or media room, a bedroom, or media library.

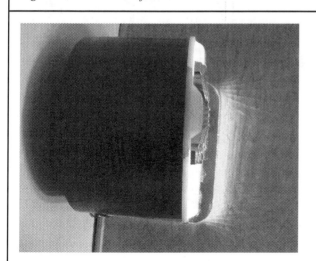

Figure 6-17. *Light effect seen from above*

In the final view (from above), you can see the light prongs radiating out. In a darkened room, these reach out quite a long way.

Summary

In this chapter, you have taken a necessarily brief look at the concept of the Smart Home and some of the history behind it. You've looked at some ideas that, for the technically-able Smart Home maker at least, can break the communications log-jam that I personally believe holds back the Smart Home from going truly mainstream.

You've looked at how to use a mixture of low-cost, easily available technologies to join up the islands of intelligence within a Smart Home infrastructure. Of course, all you have seen here is a set of individual ideas and small projects, not a detailed implementation. Nevertheless, I hope that this brief foray into this area has provided you with enough inspiration to get going on some of your own ideas!

Index

▓ W, X, Y, Z

Get the eBook for only $10!

Now you can take the weightless companion with you anywhere, anytime. Your purchase of this book entitles you to 3 electronic versions for only $10.

This Apress title will prove so indispensible that you'll want to carry it with you everywhere, which is why we are offering the eBook in 3 formats for only $10 if you have already purchased the print book.

Convenient and fully searchable, the PDF version enables you to easily find and copy code—or perform examples by quickly toggling between instructions and applications. The MOBI format is ideal for your Kindle, while the ePUB can be utilized on a variety of mobile devices.

Go to www.apress.com/promo/tendollars to purchase your companion eBook.